DURKHEIM

Gianfranco Poggi

OXFORD
UNIVERSITY PRESS

2000

OXFORD
UNIVERSITY PRESS

Great Clarendon Street, Oxford OX2 6DP

Oxford University Press is a department of the University of Oxford.
It furthers the University's objective of excellence in research, scholarship,
and education by publishing worldwide in

Oxford New York

Athens Auckland Bangkok Bogotá Buenos Aires Calcutta
Cape Town Chennai Dar es Salaam Delhi Florence Hong Kong Istanbul
Karachi Kuala Lumpur Madrid Melbourne Mexico City Mumbai
Nairobi Paris São Paulo Shanghai Singapore Taipei Tokyo Toronto Warsaw

with associated companies in Berlin Ibadan

Oxford is a registered trade mark of Oxford University Press
in the UK and in certain other countries

Published in the United States
by Oxford University Press Inc., New York

A catalogue record for this book is available from the British Library

Library of Congress Cataloging in Publication Data
Data applied for
ISBN 0-19-878087-7

1 3 5 7 9 10 8 6 4 2

Typeset in Trump Mediaeval
by RefineCatch Limited, Bungay, Suffolk
Printed in Great Britain
on acid-free paper by
T.J. International Ltd., Padstow, Cornwall

Acknowledgements

The manuscript of this book came into existence chiefly during research-and-writing stays I made at two universities respectively in 1998 and 1999: the University of Aquila and the Australian National University (Canberra). I am grateful to both institutions for the contribution made in each by colleagues and by staff to the advancement of this book. A visiting Fellowship held in Canberra at the Humanities Research Centre was particularly helpful.

After receiving his doctorate from the European University Institute, Sebastian Rinken made a very valuable contribution to my research, especially as concerns the secondary literature on Durkheim. Two current researchers at the Institute, Izabella Karlowicz and Daniel Guinea, lent further assistance on this matter. Throughout, Elizabeth Webb, a secretary at the Institute, contributed patiently and effectively to the progress and completion of the manuscript.

Contents

Abbreviations   x

1 A Scholar's Life and Its Context   1

Some Biographical Facts   1
Durkheim and His Generation   5
The Contemporary Significance of Durkheim's Work   11

2 Nature and Task of the Sociological Enterprise   14

A Positivist Manifesto   14
Philosophy as an Opponent   16
Treating Social Facts as Things   18
The Role of Sanctions   21
Observation versus Speculation   23
Types of Society   25
A Commitment to Explanation   27
Psychology as an Opponent   29
The 'Emergence' Argument   31
Individualization as a Social Process   33

3 The Pattern of Social Evolution   37

An Ecological Approach   37
How Are Societies Put Together?   39
Some Problems with This Contrast   42
Differentiation as the Master Process   44
An Alternative Construction Criticized   46
Two Types of Solidarity   47
The Social Dynamics of Change   50
An Argument about 'Representations'   52
Provisional Conclusions Concerning De la division du travail
social   55

4 Deviance   58

The Key Text: Suicide   58
Manners of Acting and Thinking   59
Suicide as Deviance   62
The Construction of Suicide Types   63

Why Deviance?   66
Egoistic Suicide   69
Altruistic Suicide   73
Anomic Suicide   76
A Critique of Modern Society   79

5 What *Is* Society for Durkheim?   84

A Missing Definition   84
A Contingent Reality   85
Two Kinds of Representation   86
Durkheim's Pathos   88
The Centrality of 'Ought'   90
Twofold Man   93

6 Law   99

Main Sources   99
Durkheim's Understanding of Law   100
Sanctions: Repressive and Restitutive   102
Crime and Punishment   103
The Evolution of Criminal Law   106
The Institution of Contract   108
The Evolution of Property   109
Further on the Law of Contract   112
The Emergence of Consensual Contract   114
Contract as a Point of Arrival, Not of Departure   116
Individual Rights in General   118

7 Political Institutions   121

The Place of Political Themes within Durkheim's Work   121
Durkheim's Political Blind Spots   123
The Differentiation of Political Structures   124
The State as Society's Brain   126
Democracy   127
Democratic Communication   129
Dangers of Democracy   131
The Political Role of Occupational Groups   132
A Corporatist Project   134
Civil Society   138

8 Religion

141

Two States of Consciousness   141
Sacred and Profane   146
Inadequate Understandings of Religion   148
Totemism   151
God Is Society   152
Society Is God   155
Rituals   157
Durkheim's Pathos Again   162
An Answer to the Pathos   164
A New Religion?   167

Notes   169
Index   175

Abbreviations

Most of the references to Durkheim's writings given in the text are preceded by a single letter, followed by the page number(s) in the French edition. These numbers are followed by numbers *in italics*, referring to the location of those passages in the current English-language editions of the same writings, listed below. The translations, unless otherwise indicated, are always the author's. References to other works are given in footnotes, wherever possible citing both the French text and the English translation.

D   *De la division du travail social*, 1892 (Paris, PUF, 1973); *The Division of Labour in Society* (New York, Free Press, 1997)

F   *Les Formes élémentaires de la vie religieuse: Le système totémique en Australie*, 1912 (Paris, PUF, 1985); *The Elementary Forms of Religious Life* (New York, Free Press, 1995)

L   *Leçons de sociologie: Physique des mœurs et du droit* (Paris, PUF, 1950); *Professional Ethics and Civic Morals* (London, Routledge, 1992)

R   *Les Règles de la méthode sociologique*, 1895 (Paris, PUF, 1977); *The Rules of Sociological Method; and Selected Texts on Sociology and its Method* (London, Macmillan, 1982)

S   *Le Suicide: Étude de sociologie*, 1897 (Paris, PUF, 1976); *Suicide: A Study in Sociology* (London, Routledge, 1989)

S&P   *Sociology et philosophie* (Paris, PUF, 1974); *Sociology and Philosophy* (New York, Free Press, 1974)

I

A Scholar's Life and Its Context

Some Biographical Facts

Émile Durkheim was born on 15 April 1858 in Épinal, a town
located in the Lorraine region of France, to Jewish parents; his father
was the last in a line of rabbis, and the household was characterized
by an austere mode of life and by devotion to learning. The sacred
learning of the Jewish tradition, and the expectation that he would
inherit his father's vocation, were rejected by Emile in his ado-
lescent years, but without a dramatic break.[1] His later relationship
to Judaism, at any rate at the conscious level, was marked by what
might be called a respectful distance; Durkheim considered Judaism
an intrinsically archaic religion, because of its exclusive concern
with the destiny of one single people, its lack of a universalistic
vocation comparable to that of Christianity. Of the latter, he
wrote: 'Everybody recognizes that the Christian religion is the most
idealistic that ever existed' (D 137; 114). But he never replaced his
native allegiance to Judaism by one to another religion; in spite of
his eloquently articulated sense that every society *needs* religion as
a set of beliefs and practices relating to a sacred realm of reality, he
subscribed to no such beliefs and engaged in no such practices.

As concerns the dominant confession in the France of his time,
Catholicism, Durkheim's expressly agnostic posture was sharpened
by a keen awareness of and aversion toward the reactionary role

played by the Catholic Church in the nation's cultural and political conflicts. These feelings were amply reciprocated by the other side: Catholic clergymen and academics never tired of evoking and deprecating Durkheim's Jewish ancestry, and of imputing to his doctrines and to his conduct as an academic leader the intent to loosen the hold of Christianity upon the minds of French children and youths, and to lead them to godlessness.[2]

The intense domestic conflicts played out in France during the central phase of Durkheim's life—the last decade of the nineteenth century, and the fifteen years preceding the First World War— echoed to some extent two overlapping tragedies which had befallen France during his early adolescence: the defeat of the Second Empire by Prussia and its German allies, and the story of the Paris Commune, of the siege of the capital by the troops of the renascent Republic, and of its fratricidal aftermath.

Both sets of events were widely interpreted as consequences of deep and abiding divisions within French society. For many decades, the most serious of these had counterposed that part of society which considered the great revolution of the previous century a positive moment in national history and a civilizational advance of worldwide significance, and that part which condemned that revolution as a betrayal of all that France had stood for. Growing up in the shadow of those consequences may have engendered that concern with the problem of division, that passion for unity, which was to inspire Durkheim throughout his life.

He completed his secondary education, so to speak, in two instalments; after gaining his *baccalauréat* at Épinal in the mid-1870s, he attended a lycèe in Paris, and gained admission in 1879 to the École Normale Supérieure, a high-grade academic institution established after the revolution for training lycèe teachers; these constituted the elite personnel within the French educational system, and were themselves educated to such standards that many of them aspired to an academic career. At the École Durkheim studied chiefly history and philosophy, and after graduation (1882) he gained a position as a philosophy teacher in a lycée. While holding this, he was awarded a fellowship to study the current condition of the social sciences in Germany (1885–6)—an experience which strengthened his intent to play a leading role in establishing sociology as a discipline within the French university system.[3]

Durkheim took a series of steps toward this aim. His first academic appointment, at Bordeaux university (1887), was to teach 'social science and pedagogy'; the latter was conventionally the field of philosophy that deals with education (and thus, as Durkheim interpreted it, also with the family, a favourite lecturing subject for him), and he went on teaching and publishing within it for years. But when the appointment became a regular chair at the same university (1895), the chair's subject was named as 'social science'. In the meantime Durkheim had published his great doctoral dissertation, *De la division du travail social* (1892), as well as a number of other writings which expressly staked out the territory of sociology as a distinctive social science (the most important of these was *Les Règles de la méthode sociologique*, published in 1895), and made available to readers the content of other courses he had been teaching in that subject. Another masterpiece, *Le Suicide*, was published in 1897, and it bore the subtitle *Étude de sociologie*.

At that time the French academic system was highly centralized (some would argue that it remains so today, though to a lesser extent), on two counts: first, university policies were to a large extent prescribed by ministerial agencies in Paris and their advisers, and promulgated and sanctioned by means of laws and by-laws; second, the academic institutions established in Paris (not just the Sorbonne, but the so-called *Grandes Écoles*) stood informally, but indisputably, at the head of the system, and exercised an unchallengeable leadership over the provincial universities, Bordeaux among others. Thus, Durkheim's intent to 'establish' sociology, both as a form of scientific discourse and as a component of the academic system, could only be effectively pursued in and from Paris itself.

Already in 1896, whole still teaching at Bordeaux, he had found a home with a Parisian publisher for a new periodical, *L'Année Sociologique*, destined for great success in the scholarly world: its mission was to review systematically each year the publications which had appeared in the previous year or two in the field of sociology, and those from neighbouring disciplines which had a bearing on sociology as Durkheim defined it. It was largely as the editor of the *Année*, by setting the journal's policy, selecting its collaborators, and commissioning and vetting their contributions, that for the subsequent twenty years Durkheim operated assiduously and efficiently (to the chagrin of his critics and opponents) as a *chef d'école*. That is, he captained a nucleus of scholars pursuing a scientific programme of his making, and, when required, operated as the boss of a powerful caucus which sought the appointment and advancement of appropriate candidates for academic positions and research opportunities.

In 1902 Durkheim left Bordeaux and moved to the Sorbonne, where he had been appointed to the Chair of Science of Education. The energy and enterprise, the intense moral commitment to his vocation, the mastery of its practice in the lecture and the seminar room, the skill in identifying, training, motivating, and promoting particularly gifted students which he had shown at Bordeaux, ensured that he continued to shine in the more exalted setting of one of Europe's oldest and most distinguished universities, and gave him the stature of a widely recognized intellectual leader. But he also lectured at other academic institutions, travelled to scholarly gatherings, continued to edit *L'Année Sociologique*, and held a privileged position as an adviser to governmental bodies and political personalities. In a third masterpiece, *Les Formes élémentaires de la vie religieuse* (1912), he revisited in a grand manner a theme which he had often entertained previously—the nature and functions of the religious phenomenon—and grounded his bold and eloquent treatment of that theme on a painstakingly acquired familiarity with a large body of sources dealing with pre-literate societies.

By that time, at the age of 54, Durkheim stood at the peak of his powers, of his reputation, and of his influence. He had largely accomplished what he had intended to do; he had given notice to the intellectual world, in France and abroad, of the distinctiveness and significance of his doctrine, both through his own writings and through those of a growing number of younger scholars, including some affiliated with disciplines other than sociology itself. There was an unmistakable note of authority, occasionally approaching complacency, in the way in which those writings, particularly those published in *L'Année Sociologique*, evaluated the contributions scholars from various European countries made year by year to a number of fields, from sociology itself to criminal law to geography to classical history. The *chef* had put in place a scientific programme of great scope, which he and his followers pursued with great industry and assurance. Opponents' charges that the body of scholarship produced by Durkheim and the Durkheimians was largely inspired by an ideological design were mentioned with disdain, if at all. In fact, Giddens remarks

While it was true that the ideological complementarity between Durkheim's sociology and victorious republicanism accounts for much of the influence which he and the *Année sociologique* exerted in French intellectual circles, it would be a mistake to see this as deriving too directly from political patronage. Durkheim never affiliated himself directly to any political party, although he maintained a close contact with his fellow *normalien* Jaurès [one of the most prominent French socialists of the time], and both influenced and was influenced by some of the leading trends in Radical Socialism.[4]

By 1912, however, the First World War was just two years away. It would brutally show how hollow was the Old Continent's claim to be the site of a superior civilization, entitled to assert its power—economic, political, intellectual—over the rest of the world. An ardent patriot (though never a chauvinist), Durkheim played a minor role in the publicistic production intended to prove Germany's responsibility for the war (he had made his only previous venture into expressly political matters with an essay occasioned by the Dreyfus affair). By that time, he was condemned to read with dismay, in the lists of the fallen in the battlefield, the names of many of his pupils and young associates in the sociological enterprise. In 1915 his own son, himself a young scholar of promise, disappeared in the course of an ill-fated military venture at the Dardanelles—a blow from which the father never recovered. He died two years later, a spent, prematurely aged man.

What was Émile Durkheim like before such misfortune befell him? Judging from what the biographical sources suggest, his chief traits were the following. A burning sense of mission, which spurred him to untiring efforts but sometimes motivated him to intolerance and unfairness toward his rivals and opponents. An enormous confidence in his own intellectual powers, in his understanding of the proper ways to put the study of human affairs on a scientific footing, in the validity of the theses which he formulated in attacking a wide range of scholarly problems. A remarkable capacity for sophisticated, persuasive argument, which he displayed both in his teaching and lecturing and in his innumerable writings. Finally, an austere sense of morality in everyday life, which, one suspects, rendered him something of a prig.

Durkheim and His Generation

The life and the intellectual itinerary of Émile Durkheim himself, summarily recounted above, constitute but one aspect of a broader episode of modern European intellectual history, whose protagonists

constitute a fairly well-defined 'generation'. Among the other protagonists likely to be known to the readers of this series, one could
mention, besides the Frenchmen Durkheim and Georges Sorel, the
Germans Georg Simmel and Max Weber, the Austrian Sigmund
Freud, and the Italians Vilfredo Pareto and Benedetto Croce.

These individuals—all males, it will be noted—grew up in the
1850s and 1860s, that is, in the heyday of the economic, political,
military and cultural hegemony of Europe over the world at large,
and derived from this circumstance a familiarity and a proud sense
of affiliation with the Old Continent, as well as a sense that its
cultural heritage needed to be further elaborated, and brought to bear
on the destinies of less fortunate parts of the globe. At the same
time, the members of this generation were aware both of the differences and the rivalries between the Continent's component parts,
the European nation-states, and of the tensions and conflicts at
work, within each state, between different strata as well as between
different ideological tendencies. This meant that, in spite of the
similarities one detects among these authors from the vantage-point
of the early twenty-first century, and in spite of their shared location
within the world of science and scholarship, the large body of work
they produced advanced different understandings of what it means
to be European or to be modern, different constructions of historical
experience, different views concerning the nature and significance of
the study of human affairs.

This diversity within the generation in question is reflected also
in the fact that when the First World War started, the members of
this generation, more or less openly and intensely, all aligned themselves with their respective nation-states; they thus perpetrated
what was to be called *la trahison des clercs*, the intellectuals'
betrayal of their presumptive commitment to the values of objectivity, impartiality, universality. But the broader historical significance
of the First World War—the sharp discounting of the Old Continent's claim to cultural and civilizational superiority, the irreversible
loss of its centrality in world affairs—affects the whole generation
and imparts to its experience an unmistakably tragic turn.

In the case of Durkheim, this is poignantly expressed in the
ghastly casualty count suffered within the next generation of French
scholars, those he had done much to select, prepare for success, and
promote. Durkheim did not see the end of the First World War; some
members of his generation survived it by a few years, others long
enough to witness the rise of Fascism (Pareto), the initial triumph of

Nazism (Freud), and the Second World War itself and its aftermath (Croce).

The tragic overtones of the First World War are due in part to its suddenness, to the rapidity with which in 1914 the institutions which had presided, in Europe, over the 'hundred-year peace' broke down, and a war of unprecedented vastness and ferocity was unleashed. Before the war, however, various members of the Durkheim generation had sensed the fragility of the Europe-centred world order, or at any rate had begun to develop a more detached and perplexed appreciation of that culture and civilization of modernity which had found in Europe its cradle and its centre of irradiation. To a varying extent and in different ways, they had articulated intellectually and given scholarly expression to an unease, a discontent, a disquiet about the modern condition, which by the *fin de siècle* a relatively large public had come to share.

A century later, we are still (or perhaps I should write: we are *again*) familiar with this state of mind, given memorable expression, a few decades back, in the dictum 'Stop the world, I want to get off'. It is a very complex state of mind, with multiple and contradictory components. Here, I would like to focus on only one of these, which according to some authoritative accounts was particularly significant for the whole Durkheim generation, and with respect to which Durkheim himself held a fairly distinctive position[5]. It consists in questioning the role of rationality in human affairs.

In the immediate intellectual milieu within which Durkheim operated, turn-of-the-century France (although the same thing can be said of Italy at the time), this theme was raised in a particularly dramatic fashion by a sustained consideration of the phenomenon of 'the crowd' (*la foule, la folla*). A small but significant body of literature, consisting both in essays for the broad cultured public and in monographs or treatises intended for scholarly audiences, discounted the role of rationality in human affairs by emphasizing the persistence among subjects at large of irrational passions, which repeatedly, under certain conditions, would find expression in forms of mass conduct characterized by their unpredictability, violence, volatility and destructiveness.

On two counts, this emphasis amounted to a critique of the modern condition, and to a worried reflection upon the 'sustainability', as we would say today, of that civilized ordering of social affairs in which modern Europe took pride. In the first place, it amounted to a rediscovery of 'the beast within', and thus to a sharp discounting of the image of the human being, the anthropology, we might say, characteristic of the Enlightenment tradition, with its emphasis on 'Man's' rational capacities. In the second place, it pointed out that certain distinctive aspects of contemporary societies—particularly industrialization and urbanization, and the attendant extension of elementary education and of some political rights to the citizenry at large—exposed the elite social groups more directly to the observation, the envy, and the resentment of 'the masses', and made more likely their unrestrained attack on civilized institutions.

On both counts, the intellectuals responsible for the *fin de siècle* (re)discovery of irrationality (Freud followed a different intellectual itinerary to a fairly similar discovery) derived from it an acute, disquieting sense of how fragile were civilized arrangements of human affairs, of how unreliable were the restraints they imposed on the dark forces lurking within the human psyche and constraining and eroding its capacity for rational discourse and activity, especially when individuals acted on a mass or collective basis.

Durkheim shared some of these concerns, but on the whole he took a rather different position concerning the irrational (or, perhaps, the a-rational) side of humanity; to put it briefly, he saw it more as a promise and less as a threat. When he discusses those breaks in the continuity of social experience whereby new waves of feeling and new visions overwhelm individuals in the presence of one another and make them act in a non-routine manner, the examples he gives by preference are not the 'murderous crowds' favoured by conservative thinkers but the imaginative deliberations of assembled political actors, energized and enlightened by an unprecedented sense of shared interests demanding to be served.

Normally, however, he was sceptical about the possibility of people building and preserving orderly arrangements for social existence on the basis of matter-of-fact discourse about circumstances and possibilities of action and reasoned agreement about what aims collective activity should pursue. The tug of contrasting interests, he felt, would inexorably disrupt such processes, or allow them only to put into place arrangements which lacked legitimacy and rested chiefly on the overwhelming pressure exerted by the favoured parts of society on others, and which were thus unstable.

Durkheim, particularly in the last phase of his work, held that the categories themselves which frame and orient all human thinking— the understandings of time, space, number, causality, etc.—are necessarily the product of unreasoned agreement obtaining within collectivities, and are generated through processes where the mythical imagination, by providing a pre-rational account of the nature, genesis, and order of things, plays a decisive, creative role. He perceived the necessarily arbitrary nature of the ways in which different cultures classified and understood things and events and thus generated each a world of its own as an orderly, meaningful ensemble. To use a current expression, he was in this manner (as well as in others, such as his understanding of deviance) a thorough 'social constructionist'.

Durkheim equally emphasized the role of ritual as a way of representing reality to individuals, in their capacity as members of a collectivity, and of reminding them of their obligations to one another, motivating and validating their compliance with existent arrangements.

Throughout his work, he also emphasized the significance of sentiments—as against matter-of-fact perceptions of reality and the reasonings referring to such perceptions—in orienting the actions of individuals. In his view, sentiments tended to become shared currents of feeling, to diffuse themselves within collectivities, with varying effects according to their contents and their intensity, sometimes unifying and energizing the collectivities, sometimes dividing and weakening them.

All three emphases—on myth, on ritual, on sentiments—led Durkheim to consider as a uniquely human asset the capacity for symbolic thinking, for positing arbitrary connections between visible and audible signs on the one hand and their referents on the other.[6] This capacity allows action—individual and collective— to orient meaningfully to realms of reality not immediately apprehensible through the senses, to pursue ends that transcend current circumstances and conditions. It allows the activation and communication of feelings which the mere ascertainment and manipulation of those circumstances and conditions would not evoke.

Above all, Durkheim considered as an indispensable component of social life at large the individual's capacity for self-renunciation, for the transcendence of one's own immediate interest, for (to employ an expression much in use today) experiencing and receiving *trust*. This is one way of interpreting an expression—the adjective 'moral'—which recurs insistently in his writings, but which he mostly did not bother to define and which he occasionally employed somewhat loosely. Most of its uses, I think, implicitly contrast 'moral' with an adjective which Durkheim himself, so far as I know, did not use—'instrumental'. In keeping with Kant's vision of morality, Durkheim considered essential human beings' capacity for relating to one another not instrumentally, as means, but morally, as ends—that is, as intrinsically valid constraints upon their own activities.

This evaluation of human potentialities which others in his time considered dispensable or even negative led Durkheim to adopt an appreciative, at times almost reverent, attitude toward aspects and moments of historical experience—pre-literate societies, the European Middle Ages—which evoked in many of his contemporaries a disdainful sense of superiority. From such situations, he felt, modern European society had much to learn; their institutions were not just worthy of respect, but could sometimes provide models for a critical reconsideration of modernity and for a serious attempt to remedy its failures and transcend its limitations.

On all these counts, one can reasonably attribute to Durkheim a view according to which (to use an expression common in his own times) 'modern man needs a supplement of soul'. But in others that view was (and is) often associated with a wholesale rejection and deprecation of modernity, a refusal to acknowledge its advent as a human advance, even at times an outright condemnation of rationality itself. Durkheim did not share these attitudes. His standpoint was throughout that of a man of science, committed to the view that reason should and could objectively ascertain, criticize, improve social conditions; he espoused the progressive import and the permanent validity of the great conquests of modernity—the development of science itself, the widening of its scope from natural to human affairs, the recognition of a growing range of entitlements of individuals, their wider involvement in the management of public activities, the growth of literacy, the decreasing cruelty in the punishment of criminal activities.

There are some aspects of what one can summarily characterize as an 'old fogey' mentality in Durkheim's writings, for instance, in the way they portray women; and, arguably, over time they develop increasingly conservative overtones. However, the reservations they express on 'the project of modernity' do not amount so much to a condemnation of it as to an exploration of its limits. Of course this entails, as I have suggested, a keen appreciation of human potentialities which that project, in its overestimation of rationality, had

unduly neglected or slighted. But Durkheim sees them as complementary to the aspects central to the modern project, and as such
they throw a new light on it, and do not radically devalue it. This, at
any rate, is the import of some of the most significant writings on
Durkheim published in the last few decades, which balance out
(sometimes, one feels, overly so) the earlier prevalent view of
his work as a wholesale critique of modernity, and as thoroughly
conservative in its political and ideological implications.

The Contemporary Significance of Durkheim's Work

Today, a century or so after the publication of the main writings to
which Durkheim's intellectual legacy was entrusted, its intellectual
significance is a matter of controversy. A few decades ago, it was
strongly contested, ironically within sociology itself, chiefly by radical authors who, knowingly or not, resurrected an old charge, to the
effect that Durkheim was 'a watchdog of the bourgeoisie'. In its new
version, the charge rested largely on the fact that the American sociologist Talcott Parsons, a dominant figure within the discipline at
that time, had drawn extensively on Durkheim in elaborating a body
of theory which, in a sophisticated and complex manner, gave priority to what he called 'the problem of social order', and proposed a
solution of it based on the sharing of 'beliefs and values' by social
actors, individual and collective. Radical writers saw this conception as intrinsically conservative, and perhaps reactionary, and
counterposed to it a variety of views drawing chiefly, instead, on
Karl Marx (and sometimes on Max Weber). Their negative evaluation of Durkheim was confirmed *a contrario* by the very positive
evaluation put forward by Robert Nisbet, an influential (unduly
influential, in my view) and avowedly conservative historian of
social thought. However, at that very time, and partly for that
very reason, the standing of Durkheim was high within the neighbouring discipline of anthropology, which had not yet had its radical,
Marx-inspired season.

By the early 1970s, however, a more sophisticated and appreciative view of Durkheim's legacy had emerged within sociology itself,
largely thanks to two moderately radical British sociologists,
Antony Giddens and Steven Lukes. Giddens[7] produced a number of
writings which assessed the contributions made by Marx, Weber,
and Durkheim himself both to our understanding of modern society

and to our conceptions of society at large; the assessment was discriminating and demanding, and gave full marks to none of those authors (chiefly because modernity had, so to speak, moved on from the time they had written). But it did much to establish that Durkheim (in particular) was well aware of the necessity that the historical novelty of modern society be matched by equally novel institutional arrangements. Lukes, in a massive and thoroughly documented yet readable and persuasive account of Durkheim's life and work,[8] conveyed a sophisticated view, in particular, of his political interests and positions; emphasized his liberal allegiances and his socialist sympathies, and made it impossible to assign him straightforwardly to the conservative camp, at any rate in the context of the French Third Republic.

Jointly, these two works did much to clear the field, both in the English-speaking world and in France itself, for a sustained wave of new Durkheim studies, not obviously inspired by an ideological prejudice for or against him. Since then, these studies have yielded, on the whole, a new, positive appreciation of the significance of his work, including its political aspects—witness, for instance, a British work entitled *Radical Durkheim*.[9] The strong current of feminist sociological work of the later part of the century, in the United States and Canada, in Britain, and on the Continent, found an easy target in Durkheim's 'essentialist' view of gender differences;[10] but even some writings sharing this inspiration have lately contributed to that new appreciation.[11] In the mid-1990s, a young social theorist published an article entitled 'Useful Durkheim', which gave pointed expression to that appreciation and replied to an earlier, dismissive essay by Charles Tilly, 'Useless Durkheim'.[12] Of course, the new appreciation was also assisted by the marked deterioration in the standing of Marxism as a form of social theory—although it probably cannot be said of Durkheim, as it can be said of Tocqueville, that the 'Fall of the Wall', in 1989, caused a sharp rise in his stock.

The renewed appreciation probably has more to do with more narrowly social-theoretical developments within both sociology and anthropology. For instance, the new contemporary emphasis on the significance of the symbolic and ritual components of social life led to a positive re-evaluation of Durkheim's seminal writings on these themes, for instance in the work of Erving Goffman.[13] Kai Erikson, an early American proponent of the so-called *labelling* theory of social deviance, drew extensively on Durkheim in *Wayward Puritans*, a path-breaking study of a major witch-hunting episode in seventeenth-century New England.[14] An Italian work on social movements, Alberoni's *Movement and Institution*, imaginatively revisited Durkheim's insights into the creativeness, and the unavoidably transient character, of 'strong states' of collective consciousness.[15] Another British work, by David Lockwood, produced novel insights into the respective strengths of Marx's and of Durkheim's theoretical legacies, a theme which had never before been treated in such depth.[16] Recently, Durkheim's writings have been called upon to contribute to the theoretical debate on liberalism and communitarianism, and considered in the same context as those by Rawls, Walzer, MacIntyre, and Rorty.[17] The contemporary awareness of the social significance of culture has been assisted by a revisiting of some of Durkheim's contributions to this theme.[18] Finally, significant reconsiderations and re-evaluations of Durkheim's legacy have been conducted in the framework of important, original reviews of the tradition of modern Western social theory, such as those undertaken by Jeffrey Alexander or Richard Muench.[19]

Contributions of this nature require, among other things, a concentrated attention to specific components of the Durkheimian *corpus*, their sources, their theoretical implications, the alternative understandings of their topics. This book does not attempt an effort of this kind. More modestly, it seeks to provide a relatively brief, selective overview of Durkheim's work, focused on his most significant writings, and does not systematically discuss the evaluations, elaborations, and criticisms of them which contemporary literature of a specialist nature continues to offer.

We can begin our task, rather conventionally, by considering in the next chapter how Durkheim construed and justified his own life project: the development of a new, scientifically grounded understanding of social reality, self-consciously embodied in a distinctive, intellectually rigorous discipline—sociology.

2

Nature and Task of the Sociological Enterprise

A Positivist Manifesto

In 1895 Durkheim published a book, *Les Règles de la méthode sociologique* (2nd edn. 1901), in which he confronted at some length a theme he had previously discussed in shorter form (as he was to do on a number of later occasions). In this chapter I consider *Règles* primarily as intended to draw a sharp boundary between social science and other modes of discourse concerning social affairs.[1]

Durkheim's argument reflects his adherence to an epistemological understanding of sociology which is generally labelled 'positivism'. As the following passage suggests, he did not particularly care for the label, which to him signified a metaphysical rather than a scientific mode of discourse; but he associated himself with what one might call the positivist project, by stating the following:

Our main objective is to extend to human conduct scientific rationalism, by showing that, considered in the past, such conduct can be reduced to relations between cause and effect, and that an equally rational operation can subsequently transform those relations into rules of action for the future. That which others have called our positivism is nothing but a consequence of this rationalism. (*R* p. ix; 33)

Whatever Durkheim's reservations on the expression 'positivism', I suggest we understand by it a nineteenth-century intellectual project which sought to bring to bear systematically on socio-historical reality the distinctive intellectual resources and strategies which, over the previous few centuries, had fostered the development of the natural sciences. If this is accepted, then *Règles* may be considered a kind of manifesto of the positivist project: that is, a particularly forthright and self-conscious statement of it, intended to clear the ground of alternative projects, to generate consensus about its own validity and viability, and to give would-be adherents to the project some general indications on how to foster its advance.

Règles is arguably the most dated of Durkheim's major writings: not for nothing, some years back, did Anthony Giddens feel called upon to publish his own *New Rules of Sociological Method*, both acknowledging the significance of Durkheim's own methodological statement and suggesting that it was obsolescent.[2] The positivist project, understood as above, still has a great number of practitioners, in sociology and in other social sciences, but most of them prefer not to acknowledge explicitly the project itself, since by the end of the twentieth century the expression 'positivism' had acquired something of a bad aura, and in many circles had become almost a *Schimpfwort*, an expressly disparaging term ('I am a social constructivist; you are a realist; he is a positivist'). In fact, even out-and-out supporters of the project might be embarrassed by some aspects of Durkheim's own formulation of it, and particularly his insistence that one can and must sharply distinguish, among various traditions and practices of discourse on social affairs, between those which are scientific and those which are not.

A related text, the opening chapter of Durkheim's *Socialisme*[3]—a book (more precisely, the text of a course of lectures) on socialist doctrines—is particularly explicit (and, to my mind, particularly embarrassing) on this count: it unproblematically places those doctrines outside the domain of scientific discourse on social affairs, conceding to them only the status of objects, not of sources (however inadequate) of such discourse. For Durkheim, socialist doctrines stand in relation to the *real* state of affairs they deal with as symptoms of it, not as analyses and interpretations concerning the validity of which one might seriously interrogate oneself. As he writes in *Règles* itself, sociology must deny any 'scientific value' to such theories as individualism, communism, or socialism, 'for they tend directly, not to express facts, but to reform them' (*R 140; 160*).

As it concerns *Règles*, one may be similarly disconcerted by Durkheim's assumption that phenomena under social scientific investigation can and must be straightforwardly defined once and for all *in limine operis*. He appears unaware of the arguments, developed in his own time, in Germany, by neo-Kantian philosophers, to the effect that 'the constitution of the object of knowledge' is a complex, demanding, and to an extent unavoidably contestable operation. And, in the light of what we have learnt since his time about the unavoidable conceptual and theoretical component of scientific observation, we may find naive Durkheim's disapproval of a certain mode of discourse because 'it goes from ideas to things, not from things to ideas' (*R* 16; 60).

But we should not overstate Durkheim's distance from what we might consider a more sophisticated and nuanced appreciation of the peculiarity of the scientific enterprise. Within the first few lines of chapter 2 of *Règles*, for instance, we find him acknowledging that all religion contains intuition about the nature of physical phenomena which go beyond the simple perception of them, in the direction of 'prenotions' of a quasi-scientific nature; and that 'reflection predates science, which merely makes a more methodic use of it' (*R* 15; 60).

In any case, once one discards various indications of what appears, from a contemporary perspective, a certain naivety and rawness in Durkheim's version of the positivist project, *Règles* remains significant as a particularly forthright and authoritative statement of it. As I have already indicated, it relies significantly on an opposition between what the project is to yield—that is, science, and again science following the natural science model—and what it rejects as inadequate, or at any rate as amounting to an intellectual enterprise to which Durkheim does not intend to contribute.

Philosophy as an Opponent

As I have indicated, in *Socialisme*, this 'Other', with respect to the intellectual product Durkheim aims for, is constituted chiefly by ideological statements criticizing the existing state of social affairs and proposing a reform of them. In *Règles*, the 'Other' is chiefly a philosophical mode of discourse about social reality (though occasionally he mentions also, as alternatives to science, 'art'— that is, a mode of knowledge oriented exclusively to the attainment of practical results, rather than to the ascertainment of states of things—as well as views based purely on commonsensical assumptions). Note that the philosophical discourse Durkheim opposes sometimes does not recognize itself as such, and characterizes itself instead as scientific, and indeed sometimes as expressly sociological. However, for Durkheim practically all that had gone under the name of 'sociology' before him did not deserve that label, because it was in fact philosophical in nature; this, in his view, applied most clearly to the writings of Auguste Comte, and to a somewhat lesser extent to those of Herbert Spencer.

At one point in his life, Durkheim, asked by someone why, after receiving a thorough philosophical training, he had abandoned that discipline, answered: 'In philosophy you can say *anything* you want.' (He continued, however, to contribute to philosophical journals and to attend philosophical conferences.[4]) *Règles* reflects and articulates the same reason for that choice. That is: philosophical discourse about social affairs is essentially arbitrary and boundless, not being disciplined and constrained by a systematic empirical reference. (Durkheim, however, would not, in this context, use the term 'empirical', which in the academic vocabulary of his time denoted an unsophisticated, trial-and-error approach to knowledge.) It projects, and subsequently moves within, a discursive realm composed purely of conceptual entities.

Instead of observing things, describing them, comparing them, one is content to become aware of one's ideas, to analyse them, to combine them. Instead of a science of realities, one creates no more than an ideological analysis.   (*R* 15; 60)

Accordingly, the philosophical approach to social affairs tends to take as its concern the essence of this or that phenomenon—say, of marriage, or of law—and to ignore the variety of arrangements covered by each concept. Furthermore, such discourse has a built-in tendency toward normative argument: it tends to privilege questions about how things should be, rather than what they are. Thus, it assumes and validates, in its own fashion, moral and sometimes political preferences of which often the philosophers themselves are not aware. Moral philosophers in particular—but this is a propensity they share with economists—sometimes proclaim 'laws' which, unlike 'true laws of nature', do not disclose the relationships obtaining between facts, but merely convey how one thinks they *ought* to be connected (*R* 26–7; 68–9).

Treating Social Facts as Things

On the other hand, the first commitment of science, *qua* science, is to ascertain states of fact, not to discourse about purely mental objects; and states of fact cannot be ascertained except through observation. This should hold for social science, too; for its identity as a distinctive and worthwhile intellectual project, capable in due course of matching the achievement of the natural sciences, is ultimately grounded on the objective existence of a realm of facts— *social* facts—which it should make its own business, first and foremost, to observe.

Durkheim formulated this principle, sharply and controversially, as follows: social facts should be considered *as things*. The expression I emphasized—in French, *comme des choses*—lends itself to two interpretations. In one, they should be treated *as if they were* things. In the other, they should be treated as things because that is what they *are*. Durkheim stands by the second interpretation. 'Social phenomena are things and are to be treated as things' (*R* 27; 69). For reasons we shall see later on, they are things *sui generis* (a favourite expression of his), that is, things unlike any other things; but they share with those other things, we might say, 'thing-hood', and on that account, not just as a fiction or as a methodological preference, should be treated as things.

This principle is controversial because on the face of it it neglects a distinctive, remarkable aspect of social facts. Take as an example of these, say, the prohibition of incest, or a language system: both these phenomena are not facts of nature, but human products; they exist as a result of agency. The awareness of this peculiarity grounds two tendencies of philosophical thinking deplored by Durkheim: first, assuming that in order to discourse about them it suffices 'that we become aware of ourselves, in order to know what parts of us we have placed in them and how we have put them together' (*R* p. xiv; 37); second, allowing that discourse to reflect our preferences and evaluations, rather than the givens of reality.

Durkheim concedes that social facts become such through human agency (*R* p. xv, 18; 38–62), but denies that this authorizes those two tendencies. For that agency does not rest with the individual who seeks to philosophize about those social facts. In the first place, it has been exercised in the past—for instance, the language he/she uses to think and discourse has emerged since time immemorial. In the second place, agency has not been exercised by an individual, but by a collectivity, and on behalf of collective, not individual, purposes. (The example of language is again apposite.)

On these two points Durkheim grounds the first of two characteristics of social facts that establish their 'thing-hood': they are external with respect to individuals, constitute givens with respect to their acting and thinking. The second characteristic is that things (and social fact as things) are not simply *there*: they also exercise a pressure on action, make a difference to the way it would unfold in their absence. Action in its flow encounters social facts as a stubborn resistance; attempts to think them away, to act as if they were not around, yield frustrating results. 'Far from being the product of our own will, social facts determine it from outside; they are something like a mould into which we are obligated to pour our actions' (R 29; 70).

Règles phrases this point by suggesting that social facts (*qua* things) constitute a 'constraint' on action; but the noun Durkheim chooses (*contrainte*) has connotations not only of constraint but also of compulsion. The Preface to the second edition, in fact, speaks of their possessing a 'coercive power' on individuals, exercising on individual consciousnesses a 'coercive influence' (R p. xx; 43). It denies, however, that *contrainte* thus understood constitutes, as it were, the essence of social facts, that coerciveness is the sole or the dominant relationship they possess in relation to individuals. Rather, it is a feature of them by which they can be identified in reality, constituted into a specific field for scientific observation, classification, analysis.

A prime complex of social facts which, two years before *Règles*, Durkheim had discussed in *Division du travail* is constituted by those in the next chapter which we are going to label the 'ecological arrangement' of societies. These, as Durkheim summarizes the earlier argument, comprise 'the number and nature of the elementary parts making up the society, the pattern of their arrangement, the degree of interaction they have attained, the distribution of the population over the surface of the territory, the number and nature of avenues of communication, the form of dwellings' (R 12; 57). These phenomena, which, as we shall see later, constitute for Durkheim the 'substratum' of a society and determine its 'morphology', possess the thing-like features attributed above to social facts: they 'impose themselves on individuals'. For instance:

---

we cannot choose the form of our houses any more than we can that of our clothes; at any rate, the one is obligatory to the same extent as the other. The avenues of communication determine imperiously the direction taken by internal migrations and by exchanges, and even the intensity of those exchanges and migrations, etc. (*R* 13; *58*)

Yet Durkheim goes on to say that in fact those phenomena inscribe themselves into material reality only through the operation of others which are in turn thing-like but 'extremely immaterial': *manières d'agir et de penser*, 'ways of acting and thinking'. As is clear from *Règles* but even more clear from the Preface to the second edition, 'ways of acting and thinking' are the social facts *par excellence*: they are the constituent elements of *institutions*, that is, of complexes of beliefs and practices pertaining to a given realm of social reality, which have become crystallized and, again, impose themselves upon individuals (*R* p. xxii; *45–6*).

Durkheim notes, however, that some modalities of activity, of thought, and of emotion impose themselves on individuals and shape their conduct without having attained institutional status; they simply communicate themselves to and through individuals, for instance those assembled in a crowd, or at a public occasion, in a particularly compelling manner. They operate like *courants sociaux*, 'social currents', which occasionally displace established and routinized ways, and sometimes replace them with different, though equally imposed and sanctioned, routines and patterns. They stand in relation to the core social facts, *institutionalized* ways of acting and thinking, as these stand to the morphological, materially embodied features of a society: they manifest themselves in them.

In Durkheim's thinking, the relations between these three orders or layers of social reality ('currents', institutionalized ways of acting and thinking, and morphological features of society) are relatively loose and contingent. Not all 'currents' eventuate in institutionalized ways, and not all of these emerge from the crystallization of 'currents'; most, in fact, develop otherwise, through a slower, less dramatic process of collective elaboration; nor do all embody themselves in the morphological features, manifest themselves in the ecological arrangement of a society. Far from it: mostly, those I have called above *core* social facts do not shape social existence via the unmistakable facticity of, say, a society's road system. They are indeed things, but not material things; they are, through and through, mental in nature, being constituted by 'representations'.

As such, they exercise on individual minds a peculiar pressure, immaterial in nature:

The pressure exercised by one or more bodies on other bodies or for that matter on wills should not be confused with that which the consciousness of a group exercises upon the consciousness of its members. What is utterly peculiar to social constraint is that it is grounded not on the rigidity of certain arrangements of molecules, but on the prestige vested in some representations. (R p. xxi; 44)

This view poses a problem for someone committed to the idea that scientific discourse on social affairs (like *all* scientific discourse) must be based on observation. All representations are lodged and processed within individual human minds (R 97; *125*)—and Durkheim never thought otherwise, though he was thought by some to adhere to the notion of a 'group mind'. For instance, 'what is a given for us is not the idea which men form of (economic) value, for we have no access to this: rather, it is the values which are actually exchanged in the course of economic relations. It is not this or that conception of a moral ideal; it is instead the complex of rules which actually determine conduct' (R 27–8; *69*).

The problem is particularly acute as concerns the peculiar quality that, above, Durkheim calls 'prestige'. If it is distinctive to social facts, and if, as he writes, that quality attaches only to some representations as against others, how are we to know *which* ones? How can we observe the prestige in question, and thus separate those representations on which it is bestowed from others which do not enjoy it and thus presumably do not qualify as 'social facts'?

The Role of Sanctions

Durkheim answers, in this text and in others: we can objectively decide which representations, which ways of orienting one's thinking and acting, *do* so qualify, by observing whether they are sanctioned. That is: *if* society takes notice of whether some representations are complied with (followed in the concrete course of individuals' thinking and acting) or not complied with, and attaches respectively positive or negative consequences to compliance/non-compliance, *then* we are dealing with social facts; otherwise, not.

Sanction, for Durkheim, stands as a proxy for the prestige with which the representations that pass the test are endowed; it signals that, as it were, society *stands behind* them. Whether a given representation is sanctioned can be observed with greater or lesser ease according to the circumstances. Formal laws constitute only a small portion of those innumerable 'representations' which orient and discipline individuals in their everyday existence, and are sanctioned, if at all, informally. But such laws, expressly promulgated as texts by legislative bodies and policed by enforcement agencies (police units, court systems, penitentiary institutions, etc.), make the sanctioning process relatively obvious and explicit.

This is one reason for Durkheim's sustained attention to legal phenomena. As we shall see in the next chapter, *Division*, in particular, treats them as the main indicators of the contrasting natures of two basic ecological arrangements, and of the associated change in the nature of societal solidarity, from mechanical to organic. It is not just the case that the conferral of legal status on some prescriptions marks them particularly visibly as social facts; furthermore, the sanction can be provided by different kinds of laws, and this produces a visible difference among the social facts themselves. *Règles* recapitulates this approach: 'we have studied social solidarity, its different forms and their evolution, on the basis of the system formed by the juridical rules which express those forms' (*R 45; 83*).

Another possible reason for Durkheim's attention to legal facts is that for a modern society laws constitute a particularly appropriate way of effecting institutional change, of abolishing or introducing social arrangements, according to whether they have been retarding and impeding, or favouring and promoting, needed developments. This is a task for social science, which in the positivist project was not meant to be an end in itself, but, in its mature state, an instrument for conscious control over social affairs and for improving the human condition. 'There ought to be a law' is a frequent and banal comment on situations one would like to see mended or eliminated. One might easily imagine Durkheim himself making such a pronouncement, but not without stating or implying that he had scientifically ascertained on the one hand that a given situation should and could be remedied, and on the other how this ought to be done. His repeated and articulate pleas for conferring public faculties and responsibilities on occupational bodies, which we will consider in the next chapter, are significant exemplars of this kind of argument.

The strategy of inferring that a given representation is a social fact from the observable fact of its being sanctioned privileges, as I have said, formal juridical rules as against other representations, less visibly and publicly sanctioned. But, more broadly, it privileges relatively stabilized, routinized, institutionalized expectations, whether legally or otherwise sanctioned, and gives lesser status to pre-institutional phenomena, and particularly to those which, as we have seen, Durkheim characterizes as *courants sociaux*, 'social currents'—states of opinion, diffuse and changeable collective emotions, orientations of taste and judgement, which affect individuals, and impose themselves on them, without being backed by sanctions, legal or otherwise. Evidence for these *courants* can, however, be drawn from the shifts they produce in visible collective practices; the latter, in particular, leave their mark on social statistics, particularly those pertaining to crimes and other forms of deviance, but also those concerning, say, the volume of market transactions, or changes in public preferences concerning fashion and other modes of consumption.

Observation versus Speculation

Thus, in the social realm, observation—the grounding practice of science—can be targeted on a number of diverse objects: 'Law exists in law codes, the movements of daily life inscribe themselves in statistical figures, in historical monuments, fashions in modes of attire, tastes in works of art' (R 30; 71–2). This very diversity of the social and of its observable evidence imposes on its student a further practice: delimiting expressly and sharply the specific social phenomenon he/she intends to study, by means of a definition of it based, again, on observable traits. Durkheim recommends this with an emphasis one may find baffling, but which is directed against two alternative practices: on the one hand, unproblematically presuming that one more or less knows what one talks about when one selects for discussion a given phenomenon (be it e.g. crime, religion, or marriage), so that an express definition of it is dispensable; on the other, adopting a definition that claims to express immediately the nature of a phenomenon, instead of determining it on the basis of empirical givens.

Science, in order to be objective, must take its departure not from concepts whose formation has preceded it, but from sense data; from these must be directly drawn the components of its initial definitions . . . It needs concepts which convey adequately things as they are, not as it is convenient to conceive of them for practical purposes ... Thus, it must create new concepts, and in order to do so, leaving aside common notions and the related expressions, must go back to sensory activity, the prime and necessary basis of all concepts. (R 43; *81*)

Durkheim particularly stresses the necessity to refer back to sensory data, if only as the point of departure for an intellectual activity seeking to transcend them, when he debates the standard approach of philosophers who deal with morality. Normally, they reduce all of it to aspects of one single moral principle or unitary system of principles, apprehended through sheer conceptual effort.

Thus, all questions which ordinarily ethics poses to itself are led back, not to things, but to ideas; what it matters to know is what in essence is the idea of law, or the idea of morality, not the nature of law or of morality taken in themselves. Students of morality have not yet learned to observe this simple principle: in the same way that our representations of sensory things come from the things themselves and express them more or less precisely, our representation of morality originates from our awareness of rules which operate before our eyes and gives a schematic presentation of them. As a consequence, the matter of science is represented by those rules and not by our summary view of them, in the same way that physics takes as its object bodies as they exist, not the idea of them entertained by people.   (R 23–4; *66*)

One implication of this refusal to confront the facts of morality 'on the ground' is that the student is unable to recognize their variety. It is not just the case that morality comprises a multiplicity of rules valid for different phases and aspects of social life; the point is that the rules applying to a *given* phase or aspect vary, sometimes drastically, from one context to another. Thus the range of variation, from which one can learn a great deal about not just morality but the contexts themselves, is instead neglected, and one discourses about a phenomenon in hopelessly generic terms.

    An index of this is the tendency of moral philosophers, or of other students, sometimes defining themselves as sociologists, to consider *l'humanité*, humankind, as the ultimate referent of their arguments. Durkheim has little use for this tendency, and the related tendency to speak of 'the evolution of mankind' in equally generic terms:

One can make [of such evolution] the object itself of inquiry only if one posits it as an intellectual construct, not as a thing. Actually, it is so much a purely subjective representation that, in fact, the progress of mankind does not exist. What does exist, and alone offers itself to observation, are particular societies which are born, develop, die, independently of one another. (R 20; *63–4*)

Types of Society

On the other hand, Durkheim dissociates himself from the opposite tendency, typical of historians, to emphasize exclusively what is peculiar to each society, to acknowledge human variety to such an extent that it becomes impossible to formulate any generalizations holding across some, let alone all, societies. The *via media* recommended in *Règles* aims, we might say, at bounded variety. That is, it elaborates *types* of society, under each of which can be subsumed a number of individual, historically given societies, similar enough that any one of them can be considered primarily as an embodiment of a given type. In order to identify types without again falling into the trap of giving priority to an 'idea' characterizing each, the recommended strategy, already followed by Durkheim in *Règles*, gives priority to what he calls morphological considerations.

We know . . . that societies are composed of parts added to one another. Since the nature of each compound necessarily depends on the nature and number of the composing elements and on the manner they are combined, these are obviously the features we have to start from; and in fact we shall see, subsequently, than on these depend the general facts of social life. On the other hand, since they are morphological in nature, one could label *social morphology* that part of sociology whose task it is to establish and classify social types. (80–1; *111*)

We may note in passing that this is a rather rigid way of conceiving that task, assuming as it does that it can be performed once and for all, and does not depend in principle on the nature of the problem under investigation. In any case, as Durkheim handles it, this approach to type-making allows the recognition of some variety within each type (and thus the construction of subtypes). For instance, a lengthy passage from *Règles* (R 82–88; *113–117*), carefully differentiates the prime type of very simple society worked out in *Division* into several subtypes, and terminates in an express *règle*:

One should begin, in classifying societies, from the extent to which they are composite, and take as point of departure a perfectly simple or single-segment society. Within each of the resulting classes, one should distinguish different varieties according to whether or not the initial segments coalesce completely. (R 86; *115*)

Durkheim also suggests that to the morphological differences between the subtypes correspond differences in other aspects, such as the way in which a given society symbolizes itself:

25

If, for example, [a given human group] conceives of itself as having been generated by an animal of which it bears the name, that is because it constitutes one of those particular groups one calls clans. When the animal has been replaced by a human ancestor, this is due to a change in the nature of the clan. If, over and beyond local and kinship deities, it projects other deities on which it depends, this is because the local and kinship groupings making it up are in the process of coalescing and uniting, and a religious pantheon will be a unitary one to the extent that the society as a whole has become one. (R pp. xvii–xviii; 40–1)

Whatever its strengths and weaknesses, this approach to sociological type-making is associated in Durkheim with a very keen sense of what one may call the contextuality of social phenomena, the extent to which their significance depends on the setting in which they occur (and which they concur in determining). We may find monogamy, he argues, for instance, in Règles, both in very simple and in very developed societies: but in the former case it may be a de facto phenomenon resulting from population scarcity, while in the latter it is likely to be the product of expressly promulgated norms and of strongly entertained moral preferences (R 37–8; 77).

Furthermore, whether a given social condition should be considered 'normal' or 'pathological' will also depend on the context in which it occurs. Basically, one should attach the first label to conditions occurring in the majority of cases; the second, to those occurring in a minority of cases. (In other words, what is normal is what is average.) But one must count occurrences only within sets of cases sharing the same type or subtype, and also verify that the cases in the set correspond more or less to the same stage of development of a given type or subtype. If these precautions are taken, once more the judgement 'normal/pathological' can be formed on an objective basis, instead of leaving it to philosophical reasoning or to common-sense views, with their explicit or implicit moral preferences.

Let us make clear an implication of Durkheim's sense for the contextuality of social phenomena: the tendency to see them as internal to a given context implies a preference for accounting for each phenomenon by appealing to causes which are also internal to that context. Put briefly, Durkheim prefers to explain phenomena *from within* a given context rather than *from without*, and objects to the opposite strategy that, in his own wording, seeks to *tirer le dedans du dehors* ('derive what is inside from what is outside', R 119; 142). We may label this preference 'internalist', and it is strongly articulated in the following statement: 'The prime origin of every social process of some significance must be sought in the constitution of the internal social context' (*milieu social interne*) (R 111; *135*).

I find this a rather constraining preference. Some major developments of great interest to Durkheim lend themselves to interpretations which adopt instead an 'externalist' strategy. For instance, one may account, say, for the development of property or of political organization within a previously barely differentiated, settled, peaceable society by pointing to the forcible takeover of its territory by nomadic warriors from another society and the consequent 'superimposition' of its members on those of the local population. Such interpretations tend to overgeneralize (as does the so-called *Überlagerungstheorie*) and to that extent are in turn constraining; but Durkheim seems to consider them simply as irrelevant distractions, and fails on give adequate weight to those instances, few or many, where they might indeed be on target.

In the last chapter of *Règles*, 'Rules Concerning the Administration of Proof', Durkheim spells out an implication of his own emphasis on type-making: the importance of variation and the strategic methodological significance of comparison. If contexts vary, it is important to capture their variation through type- and subtype-making, and associated with that are other significant variations, both between and within types and subtypes; all these must be expressly taken on board. 'Comparative sociology is not a particular branch of sociology; it is sociology itself, as soon as it ceases to be wholly descriptive and aims at accounting for facts' (R 137; *157*). Systematic comparison between different contexts as to the presence or absence of given phenomena, and the form they take in each, if any, constitutes a viable approximation to the experimental method, which has produced such impressive results in the natural sciences but is so arduous to replicate with respect to human affairs. Within two years of *Règles*, *Suicide* was to give the measure of Durkheim's self conscious, persistent, and skilful commitment to ascertaining the variations presented by social phenomena and comparing them systematically.

A Commitment to Explanation

This practice bears critically on a final aspect of Durkheim's view of scientific as against philosophical argument. Science is intrinsically concerned with explaining the facts to which it refers, and tends to do so by establishing cause-and-effect relationships. Philosophical argument, in so far as it deals in explanation, tends to emphasize 'final causes', that is, to attribute the existence of a given phenomenon to its consequences. To this Durkheim objects that social phenomena are put in place by complexes of pre-existent conditions which must be clearly identified; even assuming that the consequences of their existence can be envisaged and sought by actors, those conditions need to be secured if the phenomena in question are to be reproduced. For instance,

in order to reinforce the spirit of the family where it has been weakened, it is not enough that everybody understand its advantages; one must directly affect those causes which alone are in a position to bring it about. To return to a government the authority which it needs, it is not enough to sense its necessity; one must address the sole sources from which all authority descends, that is, one must establish traditions, a public spirit, etc.   (R 90–1; 120)

If such causes cannot be put in place, things needed will not come about. Vice versa, things not needed may remain in existence as long as the complexes of causes engendering them persist. One may recognize this without denying the role which 'human needs' (R 93; 122) may play in accounting for social phenomena which impinge on them. But Durkheim tends to discount that role: 'generally, social phenomena do not exist in view of the useful results which they produce' (R 95; 123)—results which Durkheim calls 'functions', rather than 'goals', because they need not to be intended in order to occur.

In any case, one should distinguish in principle the identification of their causes from the identification of their results, whether or not these coincide with the ends-in-view of actors. This second task, however, is itself a plausible component of a complete scientific account of human affairs; for, 'if the usefulness of a fact is not what makes it be, it generally needs to be useful in order to maintain itself':

For example, the social reaction to crime in which punishment consists is due to the intensity of the sentiments which it offends; on the other hand, however, it has the useful function of maintaining those sentiments at the same intensity level, for they would be weakened if the offences made to them went unchastised. In the same way, as the social context becomes more complex and more changeable, traditions and standardized beliefs are loosened, become more indeterminate and flexible, and the faculties pertaining to reflection develop; but those very faculties are indispensable to societies and to individuals seeking to adapt to a more changeable and complex context . . . In sum, far from social phenomena having their cause in the mental anticipation of the function they are called to fulfil, this function consists on the contrary, at any rate in numerous cases, in maintaining the pre-existent cause from which those phenomena derive; the former can be more easily identified once the latter has become known. (*R* 95–6; *124*)

Psychology as an Opponent

So far, my reading of *Règles* has selected for attention one particular theme of it: the contrast it seeks to establish between the enterprise to which its author is committed—the building of a social science— and other modes of discourse on social affairs, most particularly the philosophical mode. Philosophy is an ancient, diverse, and cultur- ally prestigous enterprise, whose persistent intellectual significance Durkheim does not seek to discount; but he opposes the hold it tries to maintain on the realm of social affairs (sometimes under the usurped mantle of 'sociology'). For philosophy, by its very nature, cannot match the standards of relevance and reliability which the modern sciences have established, and which social science ought to emulate within its own realm. To assist in this task, to which he is motivated by his 'faith in the future of reason' (*R* p. ix; *33*), Durkheim presents the set of rules of method I have selectively reviewed so far, the first and most significant being that the distinctive objects of social science, social facts, are things, and should be consistently treated as such. This principle is so foreign to the philosophical approach that it renders the method as a whole 'independent of all philosophy' (*R* 139; *159*).

Règles, however, has another theme of almost equal significance, the treatment of which cuts across that of the contrast between the scientific and the philosophical approach to the study of social affairs—the contrast, this time, between sociology and psychology. Durkheim is expressly and emphatically committed to the former, and while he acknowledges psychology as a growing science, and salutes the successes it has obtained over the previous few decades— after achieving its own autonomy from philosophy—he is chiefly concerned to put it in its place, and to keep it from encroaching into the domain he is staking out for sociology: the scientific study of social facts.

The insistence with which *Règles* (together with numerous other writings of Durkheim's) raises the topic of how these two disciplines relate to one another reveals its intensely problematical nature, which results from Durkheim's own understanding of social facts. As we have seen, these are, at bottom, *manières d'agir et de penser*— representations, realities 'extremely immaterial' in nature (*R* 90; *120*), carried around in people's minds, and individual minds at that, for there are no other. But psychology, as it happens, means 'the study of mind': it expressly devotes itself to the study of mental processes. Thus, how can it be kept from encompassing the study of social facts?

According to Durkheim, it definitely can and should. For the *manières d'agir et de penser* constitutive of the social realm are mental realities—mental processes, perhaps, if we think of them as connections firing in sequence between neurone sites in the brain— of a distinctive nature with respect to other similar events generated, processes, entertained within *the same* minds. In various writings, he presented an argument concerning the internal constitution of the individual itself—that is, the central object of psychology itself, which *Règles* characterizes as 'the science of the individual' (*R* 111; *135*).

Durkheim's argument, for which he used the Latin label *homo duplex*, is that by nature 'man is twofold'. The mental processes distinctive to the human species necessarily unfold within an individual mind. But the complex constituted by the representations occurring within it is traversed by a duality: some of these representations are collective in nature, for they do not originate from those minds considered singly or, as it were, considered one next to the other. Rather, they result exclusively from the co-presence and interaction of multiple minds, through processes set in motion at the behest not of those minds taken singly, but of a totality emerging from their coalescence. The collective origins, and the collective functions, of these representations are—once more—signalled by a specific quality: they are sanctioned.

We have already considered the sanction as a marker by reference to which social facts can be recognized in their factuality, taken objectively into account and, as it were, protected from philosophy's tendency to think them up and think them away, to fashion them, to make them appear and disappear at its own will. In the context of the arguments in *Règles* concerning the relation between sociology and psychology, the sanction—that is, the expectation attached to a particular representation that the compliance/non-compliance with it of the individual holding it will be taken notice of by the collectivity, respectively rewarded or punished—excludes that representation from being, so to speak, at the disposal of the individual in whose mind it is entertained, from being wholly his or her private matter, for him/her to take or leave as he/she pleases. The sanction operates to standardize minded activity across individuals, induces them, so to speak, to transcend themselves, to operate as other than wholly, unreservedly individual centres of action, responsive exclusively to their own private preferences. In sum, it de-individualizes individuals.

This is only possible if, and to the extent that, sanctioned representations originate from a reality which constitutes an Archimedean point with respect to the individuals themselves. 'As their key feature lies in the power they possess of exercising a pressure on individual consciousnesses from outside, this is due to the fact that they do not derive from them' (R 101; 127). The reality in question is not coterminous either with any single individual or with the sum of them understood as a pure sum, as—so to speak—one damned individual next to another.

Thus this reality cannot be the sheer resultant of the juxtaposition of individuals who are monads, totally self-sufficient and self-referring entities, with respect to one another. Individuals, unavoidably, make that reality up—remember, they are the only entities capable of human minded activity—but do so not exclusively in their capacity as individuals, not just *uti singuli*, but also *uti universi*, in the capacity of mutually belonging individuals, as participants in a reality which both comprehends and surpasses them.

The 'Emergence' Argument

The numerous passages, in *Règles* and elsewhere, in which Durkheim develops the argument above have sometimes disturbingly mystical, or at any rate metaphysical, overtones, and (as I mentioned earlier) have induced some commentators and critics to attribute to him the notion of a 'group mind'. Durkheim's own chief way of avoiding or countering such misunderstandings was to present, time after time, what can be called an 'emergence' argument, often signalled by the recurrence of his favourite expression, *sui generis* (meaning: of its own kind). For instance: 'It is undeniable that social facts are produced by a *sui generis* elaboration of psychical facts' (*R* 110; *134*).

The emergence argument draws an analogy between the individual/society relationship on the one hand and on the other, say, the relationship between the elements making up a chemical compound and the compound itself: there is nothing more to the compound than the components themselves, yet the compound has properties—we may call them 'emergent' properties—that cannot be found in the components. In that sense, it has a reality *sui generis*. In the same way, a living organism cannot be entirely resolved into its chemical constituents: it has those and in a sense nothing but those, yet somehow it also has life as the emergent resultant of their co-presence and interaction. Thus it is, again, a reality *sui generis* with respect to those constituents. Given this, it makes perfect sense to analyse scientifically the constituents and their own distinctive properties; but this analysis must recognize its own limitations with respect to that conducted, instead, at the emergent level, and dealing expressly with the *sui generis* reality to be found there, and only there.

Durkheim transfers this argument to the relationship between psychology and sociology, inviting the former, too, to recognize its own limitations. The following passage, taken from *Règles*, instances his reasoning (and gives an idea of his eloquence):

Society is not a simple sum of individuals, but the system formed by their association represents a specific reality with its own features. Undoubtedly, nothing collective can eventuate unless particular consciousnesses are given; but this necessary condition is not sufficient. What is also needed is that these consciousnesses should become associated and combined, and combined in a certain manner; it is from this combination that social life results, thus it is this combination that accounts for it. As they attach themselves to one another, as they become compenetrated and fused together, the individual souls give origin to a being, admittedly psychical in nature, but which constitutes a psychical individual of a new kind ... The group thinks, feels, acts wholly otherwise than its members would do if they were in isolation. If one begins with the latter, therefore, nothing of what goes on in the group can be understood. In one word, between psychology and sociology there is the same discontinuity as between biology and the physical-chemical sciences. (*R* 102–3; *129*)

Thus, society (or 'the group', as it is called in this particular passage) is a reality *sui generis*, and the specific scientific concern of sociology is constituted by those representations it marks with its sanction. One of the 'rules of sociological method' is that it should operate expressly at this emergent level, and look for the causes of social phenomena in the distinctive properties of their context, not in a dynamic attributed in the first place to individuals taken in isolation. 'It is in the nature of society itself that one must search for the explanation of social life' (R 101; 128). For instance, in an argument it recapitulates from Division, Règles suggests 'two sets of features which satisfy this condition most fully: the number of social units or, as we have called it, the volume of society, and the degree of concentration of its mass, which we have called its dynamic density' (R 112; 136).

Individualization as a Social Process

In discussing the sociology/psychology relation, in fact, Durkheim sometimes takes what one may call a defensive position, arguing against the possibility of a scientific takeover of the field of sociology by psychology, or by a speciality within the latter, 'social psychology'. The curtest formulation of this position is perhaps: 'Sociology is not a corollary of psychology' (R 101; 127). But sometimes he goes on the counter-attack, arguing in turn that much that goes on within an individual's psyche is, so to speak, put in place by social processes, on behalf of society itself. Indeed, the development itself of the individual as a relatively self-standing, self-referring, self-interested entity is, so to speak, authorized and promoted by society; and this process, which we could call individualization, occurs at two different levels.

At the societal level, in the course of the typical development theorized in Division (as we shall see in the next chapter), the advance of differentiation, the increased frequency and diversity of contacts and exchanges, the multiplication of settings and forms of interaction, the growing indeterminacy of collective constructions of reality and prescriptions for conduct, progressively foster individuality. Societies, that is, increasingly allow, or indeed demand, individuals to stand back from one another, to become aware of interests and capacities peculiar to themselves, to develop and activate their own distinctive potentialities, exercise control over themselves, to loosen their dependency on one another and lose their own similarity with one another. In these ways societies, as they advance, increasingly expect individuals to become individuals, to conduct themselves as such. Individualization is, in this sense, a distinctive feature of advanced societies.

Within the individual's life course something similar happens. Through education in its various forms children, thrown into society as 'barbarians', become socialized; and this process, at any rate in the context of advanced societies, increasingly makes them responsible for their own conduct and encourages them to become differentiated from one another, for instance by specializing in a particular trade as against cultivating skills and notions of a general nature. In this sense, too, the individual, whose mental processes psychology elects as its own scientific concern, is a *posterius* vis-à-vis society rather than a *prius*: he/she must be progressively taught and authorized by society to think and act as a relatively self-standing entity. In the light of this, the prospect of a science of society which makes its start from psychology, as the science of the individual mind, appears preposterous, in the literal sense of this expression, which means putting first what should come later.

Durkheim's keen sense that the opposite order of priority is the right one is conveyed also by his understanding of the respective tasks of sociology and psychology in the context of a science of education. To sociology belongs the prior, larger, and more critical task of identifying the structure of the educational institutions appropriate to a given society and the content of their message. To psychology belongs the relatively less significant task of attending to the process of education—the *how* of it, which is relatively invariant, rather than the *what* of it, which must be adjusted to the specific societal context where those institutions are to function. Durkheim himself, in his capacity as a professor of pedagogy, explored at length, in the context of French history, what we might call the co-variation of society and of educational institutions,[5] and at various points expended much effort in devising appropriate contents for the nation's educational system. (According to his detractors, both from the right and from the left, he was all too successful in this task.)

Durkheim's strong position on the autonomy (and, in a sense, the priority) of sociology as against psychology is strongly articulated in *Règles* (but also in other writings) in methodological terms, with reference to what we might call the statute and nature of the respective disciplines. But it is supported also by his critique of the positions taken by various authors on substantive issues, not necessarily with reference to the relationship between sociology and psychology. Spencer, in particular, claims to be 'doing sociology';

but Durkheim criticizes him, both—as we have seen—for in fact practising philosophy and for adopting what one might call a psychologizing programme in his would-be sociology. Indeed, Spencer claims that the key to societal dynamics lies in the individual's pursuit of his/her own advantage; whereas according to Durkheim that dynamics must go a long way, propelled by the unfolding of collective processes, before it *itself* brings the individual into existence.

In other writings, Durkheim practises the same combination of methodological and substantive critique on a French contemporary of his, the jurist and social scientist Gabriel Tarde. Tarde was wrong, in his eyes, both for venturing to ground a purportedly sociological enterprise on psychological premises—he was a major proponent of 'social psychology'—and for proposing an unacceptable account of major social phenomena. According to this account, again the individual was the locus of the prime mover of social dynamics, but this did not consist in the search for private advantage as in the utilitarian tradition, but in the innate tendency to imitate the conduct of other individuals. Bounced from one individual to another to another through imitation, practices originally peculiar to one individual become generalized over a plurality, and may even end up being adopted by the latter as obligatory.

Durkheim acknowledges that occasionally imitation may take place between individuals, but holds that it is a peripheral phenomenon, on no account to be considered as the primordial social process. In any case, the generalization of forms of conduct across a plurality of individuals thematized by Tarde is in most cases due to their intrinsically collective nature, to society conferring on them obligatory status by attaching sanctions to them, not to the spontaneous diffusion of practices through individuals imitating one another.

Durkheim's attacks on both Spencer and Tarde are aspects of a distinctive position, which some of his commentators call his 'sociologism', others his 'agelicism'. The position is that society is a real entity, with properties of its own, a genesis and a function not reducible to those of individuals, although it operates exclusively within and through those individuals themselves. 'The causes which engender collective representations, emotions, tendencies are not certain states of the consciousness of individuals, but the conditions in which the body social, taken as a whole, finds itself' (R 105; *131*).

For Durkheim, in fact, society *and* individuals are the only two human realities: 'if we discard the individual, only society remains' (*R* 101; *128*). But one may question the validity of his social ontology, the necessity of insisting on the reality of society. Marriage counsellors, to dispel the client's bafflement as to why two good people can no longer get along, will sometimes say: 'There is you. There is your partner. *And* there is the relationship.' As against this view, a statement about the family in *Suicide* is formulated as follows: 'For each spouse, the family comprehends: 1, the other spouse; 2, the children' (*S* 191; *185*). It thus expressly ignores the possibility, in general terms, that what there is to the social process other than the individuals is their relationship, or indeed the network of their relationships, rather than some overarching reality which, far from being generated by individuals, in fact generates them. Among his contemporaries, both G. H. Mead in America and Georg Simmel in Europe went much further than Durkheim in the direction of a 'relational' emphasis.

3

The Pattern of Social Evolution

An Ecological Approach

There are good reasons (including some suggested in the previous chapters) for imputing to Durkheim an essentially 'tender-minded' conception of social reality. His approach to the study of social affairs systematically privileges 'things that people carry around in their heads', and his conception of society itself, as we shall see, grounds its reality in shared understandings of what is true and proper. His strategic emphasis, in approaching a great range of problems, lies systematically on normative constraints upon action, on the pressure which moral considerations exercise, or *ought* to exercise, upon individuals' activities. This emphasis sometimes induces a relative disregard of other factors, such as the resources of individuals or other situational constraints within which they operate.

One must however complement this (to my mind, legitimate) construction of Durkheim's theoretical preferences with a reminder of a different and less salient yet persistent and significant emphasis, laid instead upon collective properties of groups that (on the face of it) have nothing intrinsically 'moral' or indeed mental about them, but result from, and express themselves in, material, hard-to-shift phenomena and processes which constitute (to use Durkheim's own expression) the 'substratum' of society. At bottom, these all have to do with the relationship between a human population and the land on and off which it lives.

I wrote above 'human population', but in principle some of the ways of characterizing the relationship and some of the reasons for emphasizing its significance apply also to other species. All biological populations, in order to maintain themselves, must somehow come to terms with their natural environment, adapting to it and/or transforming it, and the ways in which they cope with this necessity impart to them some at least of their distinctive structures, which select and stabilize some particular patterns of activity over against others.

There is a dynamic to this relationship, among other reasons because the more or less marked changes in the environment associated with the seasons (but in some cases with less predictable, longer-terms climatic shifts) de-stabilize those patterns and call forth corresponding changes in a given population's activities. Perhaps the generic expression 'environment', used above, does not indicate expressly enough that for any given species its environment is in fact largely constituted by other species. Each of these, in order to survive, must somehow relate to those other ones, perhaps competing with them for certain resources, perhaps allowing them to use its own activities as resources. It can also happen that two or more populations of the same species find themselves within the same environment and variously react to each other's presence.

The resulting processes, taking place between species and within species, are the object of a field of biology generally labelled 'ecology'. Correspondingly, a sustained concern with the form those processes acquire for human populations is the object of 'human ecology'—a scholarly pursuit carried out (not necessarily under that name) by biologists, sociologists, and social geographers, but occasionally also by historians and economists.[1]

Leo Schnore, a sociologist active within this field in the mid-twentieth century, has compellingly argued that Durkheim deserves to be counted among the most significant practitioners of human ecology.[2] His argument to this effect is chiefly grounded, quite appropriately, on Durkheim's first book, *Division du travail* (1892). However, Durkheim remained concerned with human ecology— without using the term—for the rest of his professional life: his last masterpiece, *Formes élémentaires* (1912), demonstrates most emphatically the priority in his thinking, as I have already said, of 'things that people carry around in their heads', yet argues that the very content of those 'things' is generated, and made socially compulsory (so to speak), by what we might call ecological constraints, and primarily by the pattern of settlement of a population over its territory.

In between those two works, in those numerous writings where Durkheim expressly discussed significant differences between types of society, he continued to characterize them in the first instance, explicitly or implicitly, with reference to the population/territory relation. However, *Division* remains the text where something one can reasonably call an ecological argument is articulated most explicitly; and my account of that text offers a brief reconstruction of that argument. The argument bears directly on the book's main concern—to identify and contrast societal arrangements broad and abstract enough to encompass the whole range of social experience.

How Are Societies Put Together?

Any notion of society implies, if it does not expressly state, that its referent is a composite reality, one made of a plurality of components. (Some German writings make this explicit by characterizing society as a *Rahmengruppe*, a 'framework-group', that is one composed in turn by groups.) If this is so, then it makes sense to differentiate the concept of society by asking in the first place how in a given instance those component parts relate to one another, how a given society is 'put together' from them. In Durkheim's own terms, the answer to this question determines what he calls the 'morphology' of society.

According to *Division*, there are basically two, and only two, fundamentally different answers to this question (D 148; *123*). In one case, the component parts are very similar to one another, but do not intensely and continuously interact, but rather lie (as it were) next to one another, each replicating the others' characteristic patterns of social existence; these encourage and sustain the self-sufficiency of each of the parts, and do not require them to exchange systematically the products of their activities. In the other case, the component parts are differentiated from one another, that is, they engage in activities which vary, sometimes markedly, from one part to another, but are to a considerable extent complementary to one another, for each activity can be carried out in a sustained manner only by drawing on the results of other activities. Thus the parts interact frequently, exchanging the products of the respective activities, and self-sufficiency is attained only at the level of the society as a whole, not of its parts.

The 'ecological' aspects of this basic difference in societal arrangements are clear in *Division*. In the first arrangement the society's population is divided up into 'segments', that is, units located in separate parts of the society's territory, each unit typically drawing all the resources necessary for its survival from its own part, but through activities of remarkable sameness from unit to unit. Should we survey the territory from above, we would not detect many regularly travelled paths or roads, but at most a few central points at which the units gather at relatively infrequent intervals for ritual purposes, rather than for exchanging products. Typically, the population in question would be small, and its units would each have to exploit a relatively large expanse of land in order to meet all the requirements for the survival of the individuals making it up. But those requirements would be elementary, and would be met by means of relatively simple, repetitive activities, such as the gathering of seasonal berries and fruits or hunting, carried out with the assistance of primitive technical devices and on the basis of unsophisticated skills, available, at the end of primary socialization, to the great majority of individuals. What individuals do, within a given population, to make a living varies between them at most as a function of age and gender. There is thus very little dissimilarity (and thus possible complementarity) both *between* and *within* the units in question: 'the society is formed by similar segments, and these in turn enclose only homogeneous elements' (D 152; *128*).

The population as a whole, to use a typical ecological expression which Durkheim does not employ, has found its *niche* in the environment; but that niche is tight, allows very little variation between units and over time, and basically compels the human population to adapt to the environment's natural givens (and their own patterns of change, if any) rather than shifting and modifying them through technology.

If, on the other hand, we could again survey from above the territory inhabited by a population whose arrangements follow the contrasting pattern, we would find that the settlements established by some of its units differ markedly from those of other units. Typically, some units are settled in densely inhabited towns, others in the countryside—and this particularly visible difference is associated with others. The activities carried out within towns may differ in turn from town to town; furthermore, they are diverse also within each town, and split up the local population into subunits associated with specialized productive and commercial practices. No subunit aims at self-sufficiency, but seeks rather to exchange the products of its own activities with those of others. Similar relations obtain also between town-based and countryside-based units, or between the units settled in different towns, to such effect that the population's territory, surveyed at length, appears crossed by multiple, frequent, regular traffics, conveying people, information, and goods from one part of the territory to others.

The physical structure itself of the territory reflects this, for over time it is modified by an increasingly extensive and complex network of roads or canals which supports the traffics in question. Close observation of these might reveal that the network, and the traffic it carries, is structured. In particular, certain units form local or regional clusters tied together by more intensive traffics; and, very importantly, a particular unit plays a central role in the network, that is, entertains frequent relations with all other parts of the territory, supplies them with particularly significant kinds of goods or information, and mediates the exchanges between different regional clusters.

[These societies] are constituted, not by the repetition of similar and homogeneous segments, but by a system of different organs each of which has a special role, and which are in turn formed by different parts. The social elements are not either juxtaposed to one another like the rings of an earthworm, nor enclosed within one another, but coordinated and subordinated vis-à-vis one another around a central organ which performs a moderating action toward the rest of the organism. (D 157; 132)

In sum, the side-by-side severalness of similar units characterizing a population under the first type of arrangement has been replaced in the second by another kind of severalness, characterized by the differentiation of units, by their interdependence, and thus by the much increased volume of their interactions, by the complexity of the whole they constitute together. This is only possible for a population of relatively large size, whose productive activities generate enough surplus—with respect to what is strictly necessary to keep all its components alive—to allow some parts to devote themselves to increasingly specialized tasks, which sometimes are not exclusively and immediately aimed at survival, but increase the sum total of productive resources, beginning with knowledge.

To take up the ecological metaphor of the niche again, a population whose relationship to the territory is so arranged typically finds in its environment a much less tight and constraining niche than one living under the previous arrangement (D 319; 269). Increasingly specialized bodies of knowledge and sets of technical devices allow a more intensive and diversified exploitation of natural resources and a more active and open-ended relation to the natural givens of the environment. The possibility of moving goods and information over relatively large distances (typically, a population of this kind controls an extensive territory) ties the periphery to the centre, leaving it less exposed to the vagaries of local circumstances (crop failures, for instance, or threats from neighbouring populations).

Interdependencies generate in specialized parts an interest in the welfare of each other and of the whole, and some parts specialize in identifying and pursuing such interest. Units settled in the countryside are likely to remain committed to internal arrangements of a simpler nature, but the now prevailing mode of productive activity (agriculture) is itself dependent, both for some of its inputs and for much of its output, on a relationship with the town which increasingly erodes the previously dominant orientation of productive units to self-sufficiency.

Durkheim does not mention a point which may be worth making: this second arrangement generally entails that the productive activities of individuals draw extensively on natural energies (from the muscular strength of domesticated animals to the power residing in controlled and/or expressly built bodies of water and in fossil deposits) in relation to which human beings stand in a relatively more controlling and masterful posture than toward, say, the energy streaming out of the sun, and which to an increasing extent can be purposefully tended and increased.

Some Problems with This Contrast

Given this stark contrast which Durkheim draws between two modalities of the relationship between population and natural environment, we may ask ourselves what might have been their respective referents, in *Division* or in other writings. If we search, within the course of human development, for exemplars of the first arrangement, we are compelled to refer back, on the basis of fairly scant prehistorical and ethnographic evidence, to populations which lived from gathering and hunting before the Neolithic revolution, before the development of the domestication of animals, of agriculture, and of towns, or which continued to live, in relatively remote parts of that world, without knowledge of or use for such development. Alternatively, within the cultures of populations already affected by that development, and about which we know a great deal more, we can try to identify some aspects, embodied in myth, ritual, folklore, and law, which (we have reason to believe) refer to the very distant past preceding the development, and presumably offer some pointers to 'the way we lived *then*'.

As concerns all other aspects, however, those cultures (including that prevailing in Durkheim's own times), when examined in the light of the two ecological arrangements we have derived from *Division*, are to be subsumed under the second. Thus, the book's central dichotomy suffers from a serious asymmetry: a relatively sound evidential basis exists only for the second arrangement. If we visualize the whole of humankind's experience as a single line and divide it into two portions according to Durkheim's criterion, the first arrangement would account for by far the longest portion, for the basic break, which we have identified with the Neolithic revolution, would occur only way down the line, fairly near the point at which Durkheim himself stood (and we ourselves stand). But in terms of what we know about that development, the asymmetry goes the other way: about the shortest portion of the line, the one comprising Durkheim's own society (and ours), we have by far the greatest accumulation of relatively sound knowledge. Not for nothing is a plausible designation for the earlier and longer segment *pre-history*, known to us chiefly through *conjecture* — as Durkheim himself acknowledges (*D* 152; *128*).

He tries to reassure his reader about the tenability of his arguments by invoking another source of insight—the knowledge of existing 'primitive' societies which had been accumulating steadily in Europe in the second half of the nineteenth century. But one may wonder how much stronger this makes the argument: the notion itself of the primitiveness of those societies simply postulates their similarity to prehistorical ones, and to that extent begs the question.

An associated problem with Durkheim's dichotomy is that it treats all the social conditions we know something about, those where social labour is divided on grounds other than gender and age, in a relatively undifferentiated fashion. One must subsume under it societies as different as those of classical antiquity and those of the European *ancien régime*. It cannot easily accommodate other conceptual distinctions: for instance, that between status and contract as basic ways of grounding and structuring social inequality. As Niklas Luhmann has recently argued, even at the highest level of abstraction one needs to distinguish at least three concepts to encompass the basic varieties of societal integration: segmental, hierarchical, and functional. But Durkheim merges the latter two, and thus lacks an indispensable device for conceptualizing the specificity of modernity, which Luhmann himself associates with the transition from the hierarchical to the functional mode.[3]

Differentiation as the Master Process

Durkheim's own understanding of modernity itself, in so far as it can be derived from *Division*, treats it essentially as the intensification and acceleration of the process of differentiation. One reason for his doing so results from something I wrote above: in principle, ecological problems must be solved by all biological populations, not just human ones. This suggests that the dominant perspective in biology, the theory of evolution, can be brought to bear on both kinds of population. But the theory of evolution, in turn, sees continuous differentiation as *the* master process. In its light

the division of labour begins nearly with the advent itself of life within the universe. It is no longer just a social institution originating from men's intelligence and will: rather, it is a phenomenon of general biology whose conditions, it seems, must be sought in the essential properties of organized matter. The social division of labour appears as but a particular form of this general *processus*. (D 3–4; 3)

Within nature this process operates at two levels: a relatively small number of species is progressively replaced by a larger and larger number; each of the later species is characterized by greater internal complexity, that is by a greater differentiation of parts, than that exhibited by earlier ones. In other terms, heterogeneity and complexity now reign both *between* and *within* units.

As concerns human societies, the same duality of effects is shown, in particular, by the developments affecting the family. Early on in their evolution, each family stands alone as a social microcosm; but subsequently it is obliged to transform itself. Instead of remaining an autonomous society within the larger one, it is drawn more and more into the system of social organs. It becomes, itself, one of those organs, entrusted with special functions. (D 188; *158*)

In turn, however, the family undergoes a process of *internal* differentiation, in the course of which

different functions, at first undivided and confounded with one another, slowly became separated and constituted apart, and distributed themselves between the different relatives according to their sex, their age, their relations of dependence, in such a manner as to make of each a special functionary of the domestic society . . . This division of familial labour controls . . . the entire development of the family. (D 92; *78–9*)

The import of this and related arguments for the study of human societies can be stated as follows. In the first place, as Durkheim writes in *Règles*, human development is itself an aspect of evolution at large, the aspect characterized by the highest degree of complexity (D 337; *283*). In the second place, our labelling of the two basic ecological arrangements as respectively first and second is not arbitrary: the first necessarily precedes the second, which presupposes it.

The division of labour cannot take place but within a pre-existent society . . . Labour does not get divided as between independent and previously differentiated individuals who unite and associate with one another to pool their different capabilities . . . There is thus a whole social life outside of the division of labour, but presupposed by it. (D 260; *218–19*)

Furthermore, as I indicated, one can gain some purchase on the variety of situations covered conceptually by the second arrangement by considering that differentiation is, as already suggested, a process; that is, it does not simply assert itself once and for all, but is capable of successive elaborations.

Naturally these do not alter the biological structure of the human species, which Durkheim treats as constant and uniform, but affect only the culture and structure of specific societies. As concerns the human species, the ongoing march of evolution does not assert itself through the emergence of new, biologically differentiated groupings—'races', as Durkheim calls them (D 296; *250*)—but through a given human population's ability to modify its mode of existence, including the arrangement governing its relationship to the environment, and thus through its own internal differentiation.

An Alternative Construction Criticized

Durkheim's perspective on modernity emphasizes these aspects of the more advanced stages of the differentiation process; but he is also concerned to rebuke some ways of construing that process that he considers both scientifically inadequate and politically and morally dubious. His chief target is a construction that we would today label as utilitarian, and which he himself, in a passage of *Division*, imputes to *les utilitaires* (D 263; 220), but more frequently to 'the economists' (e.g. D 148; 123).

According to this view, which Durkheim discusses chiefly in the version of it offered by the English sociologist Spencer—(although Durkheim prefers to call him a 'philosopher'), the general significance of the process, which culminates in the development of modern society, lies in removing or loosening most of the moral, juridical, and political restraints which all preceding societies had laid upon individuals' pursuit of their own private advantage. From this, according to the well-known formula according to which private vices become public virtues, derives modern society's superiority in producing wealth, generating knowledge, promoting the improvement of mores, manners, tastes.

All this results from the fact that such society prizes and rewards, instead of condemning and constraining, individuals' ability to exercise their own judgement and to develop and risk their own resources on an increasingly open market in order to obtain the best possible exchange for the products of their own activities. The differentiation process itself is treated as the result of that ability, and in its modern, advanced stages, it induces the progressive contractualization of the relationships between individuals. That is, those relations are less and less authoritatively regulated from above, by the dead hand of tradition and/or by the arbitrary will of rulers. They are instead increasingly generated and regulated by agreements between private, free and equal individuals, who generally enter them for a limited time and for express, limited purposes, and devise them according to the objective relations, revealed as such by the market, between what they have to offer to and what they need from one another. Contracts are the only form of juridical regulation compatible with an advanced differentiation process and thus with modern society itself. They ought to replace other forms of public nature, which interfere with the workings of the market.

In spite of the fact that he largely agrees with Spencer's description of the differentiation process, both in *Division* and in other works (we have seen some aspects of this argument in the last chapter) Durkheim sharply criticizes his interpretation of its causes and consequences, and the related practical implications.

The causes cannot be seen (as Spencer sees them) in the individual's pursuit of his or her advantage, for the emergence of the individual as an autonomous, self-seeking entity is itself the outcome of the process in its more advanced stages (D 263; 220). In societies without, or with minimal, division of labour, there is no place for such an entity, for the physical individual is locked into a pattern of custom which leaves no room for his/her sense of distinctiveness and for the conception or the pursuit of interests peculiar to him/her.

According to Durkheim, it is a moot question whether or not the upshot of the process is (as claimed by utilitarian thinkers) an increase in private or public happiness, and many phenomena accompanying modernization (for instance, marked rises in the suicide rate) suggest otherwise.

If the division of labour had advanced purely to increase our happiness, it would have long ago reached its outer limit, together with the resulting civilization, and both would have come to a halt ... What the mounting tide of voluntary deaths proves, is not only that there is a growing number of individuals too unhappy to bear their existence, but that the general happiness of society is on the decrease. (D 215, 229; 182, 193)

The fact that civilizational advance is a product, and a necessary product at that (D 327; 276), of the division of labour does not mean one can consider it

as a goal which moves people by the attraction it exercises on them ... as a good envisaged and desired in advance ... but as the effect of a cause, as the necessary result of a given condition. It is not a target ... which men seek to approach in order to be happier or to be better ... This does not mean that civilization renders no services; but it is not the services it renders that make it advance. It is false to consider civilization the function of the division of labour: it is merely its side-effect [*contrecoup*]. (D 327–8; 276)

Two Types of Solidarity

Instead, for Durkheim the *point* of the advance of the division of labour (and thus of civilization) is that the self-seeking activities of exchange partners engender, in a society with a developed division of labour, a new kind of social integration based on the interdependence of its parts, which he labels *organic solidarity*. The solidarity typical of a society based on what we have called the first ecological arrangement he labels instead *mechanical*, for it results automatically from the similarity existent between its parts, and from the fact that all the individuals making these up adhere strongly to the same patterns of belief, the same demanding regulations of conduct.

The most remarkable effect of the division of labour is not that it increases the yield of the divided functions, but that it renders them solidary. In all these cases its role is not that of improving or rendering more attractive the existing societies, but of making possible societies which, without them, would not exist ... The economic usefulness may be of some significance in its outcome, but this widely transcends the sphere of purely economic interests, for it consists in the establishment of a *sui generis* social and moral order. This binds together individuals who, without it, would be independent of one another: instead of developing each on their own, they conduct their efforts in concert: they are solidary, and this solidarity does not make itself felt only in the brief instances where services are being exchanged, but extends well beyond that. (D 24–5; *21*)

Furthermore Durkheim condemns the political and moral preferences associated with Spencer's misconception of the causes and consequences of the differentiation process.

For him, what he calls industrial solidarity ... being spontaneous, needs no coercive apparatus either to produce it or to maintain it ... Thus the sphere of social action would progressively shrink, having no other object than that of preventing individuals from encroaching upon and damaging one another. (D 177–8; *149*)

This view would assign a marginal role to the deliberate and express regulation of social affairs by public authorities, and an ever-increasing role to the market. But the process of societal differentiation can run amok if it is not policed; the market does not have the wondrous properties imputed to it by Spencer (or, one might note, by a number of social commentators of our own time) because there persist inequalities among individuals operating in the market—particularly those rooted in the inheritance of private ownership of productive resources—which bias and distort its operations.

Modern society should not cease to orient and control the activities of its parts, including individuals' pursuit of private advantage.

It is true that contracts play an increasing role in constructing relations between individuals: but they can only do this on condition that they are validated, monitored, and if necessary enforced by public authority, for single contracts are only made possible by the operations of an institution—contract—which is not itself of contractual origin.

> The contract does not suffice to itself, but it is possible only thanks to a social regulation which is of social origin. (D 193; *162*)

> Undoubtedly, when men are united by means of a contract, it is because, on account of the division of labour, they need one another. But if they are to cooperate harmoniously, it does not suffice that they enter into a relationship, nor even that they sense the condition of mutual dependence in which they find themselves. Additionally, it is necessary for the conditions of that cooperation to be fixed for the whole duration of their relationship. It is necessary that the rights and duties of each be defined, not only in the light of the situation within which the contract is made, but also with a view to circumstances which may arise and modify that condition. Otherwise every moment would bring conflicts and frictions ... for each contractant would seek to obtain at the least cost that which s/he needs, that is to acquire as many rights as possible in exchange for as few obligations as possible. (D 190; *160*)

> The law of contract stands there to determine those juridical consequences of out acts which we have not ourselves determined ... Resulting from numerous and varied experiences, it foresees that which we cannot foresee, regulates that which we cannot regulate, and this regulation is imposed upon us, although it is a product not of ourselves, but of society and of tradition ... From this viewpoint, the law of contract is not there simply to complement the agreed arrangements, but is their fundamental norm ... It lies at the basis of our contractual relationships. (D 192; *161*)

Thus the state, through its 'private law', must establish the institution of contract and adjust it to the changing requirements and opportunities of the modern, industrial economy. Through its 'public law' it must at the same time institute an increasingly specialized, active, and sophisticated body of administrative agencies, monitor the social process as a whole, apply sanctions to deviant actions by individuals and groups, and provide for the population at large indispensable conditions of citizenship such as education. In both ways it can assist in the full development of modern society, whereas Spencer considered the persistence and indeed the growth of the state, under current conditions, as a maddening obstacle to that development.

Division returns time and again to its central theme: the contrast between those two basic arrangements I have labelled 'ecological'. Here is one of the many formulations of that contrast:

The structure of societies where organic solidarity is preponderant is wholly different. They are constituted, not by the repetition of similar and homo-geneous segments, but by a system of different organs each of which has a special role, and which are in turn formed by different parts ... The social elements are neither juxtaposed to one another like the rings of an earth-worm nor enclosed within one another, but coordinated and subordinated vis-à-vis one another around a central organ which performs a moderating action toward the rest of the organism ... This social type rests on principles so different from the former one that it could only develop to the extent that this was weakened. In fact, individuals within it are grouped no longer on the basis of kinship relations, but on the basis of the distinctive nature of the social activity to which they are devoted. Their natural and necessary context [*milieu*] is no longer the context of birth, but the professional context. (D 157–8; *132*)

The Social Dynamics of Change

The sharpness itself of the contrast between the two arrange-ments poses the problem: how do you get from one to the other? Durkheim's criticism of Spencer, above, suggests in the first instance a negative answer: you do *not* get there on the backs, so to speak, of the private strivings and undertakings of individuals. The positive answer is expressly articulated at length in a central chapter of *Division* (book ii, ch. 2), and restated several times in later parts of the same work as well as in other writings of Durkheim's. It is again formulated in ways which, on the face of it, make no concessions, or minimal concessions, to what at the beginning of this chapter, I called his 'tender-mindedness'. Durkheim himself characterizes the answer as *méchaniste* (D 331, 336; *279, 282*), suggesting that it is strongly deterministic—'all these changes are produced mechanic-ally by necessary causes' (D 257; *215*)—and that (again) it attaches no causal significance to the ends-in-view of individuals. Thus, the answer also exemplifies a principle which, as we have seen, Durkheim was to formulate in *Règles*: social phenomena must be given social explanations.

The basic argument is simple. The causes of the transition from one type of society to the other are directly related to a population's ecological arrangement, for they have to do, at bottom, with the ratio of the size of a human population to the size of its territory. If, in a society characterized by what we have called the first arrangement, the population grows beyond the size that can be supported by the returns of an extensive, low-technology, low-energy mode of productive activity aimed at the self-sufficiency of its parts, those parts—in order to survive—must specialize their activities, make much more intensive use of existent resources or develop new ones, and exchange their specialized products with other parts. In the long run, there will result the demise of the segmental pattern of settlement, a loss of significance of the parts' territorial location, an increasingly dense and flexible network of traffics between them, and, for individuals, the increased significance of memberships and interests connected with specialized, changing skills.

All this requires 'the social matter to enter into wholly new configurations in order to organize itself on an entirely new basis' (D 159; 133).

The increase in the division of labour is due to the fact that the social segments lose their individuality, that the walls that separate them become more permeable, in a word that a coalescence occurs between them which renders the social matter free to enter into novel combinations. (D 237; 200)

The division of labour progresses the more there are individuals sufficiently in contact with one another to act and react upon one another. If we agree to call dynamic or moral density this coming together and the active intercourse resulting from it, we can then say that the advances of the division of labour are directly proportional to the moral or dynamic density of society. (D 238; 201)

But the latter is in turn strictly associated with a population's material density, that is—as I indicated—with the ratio of its size to the size of the territory (D 238; 201). And, given a territory, the sheer *volume* of the population, its absolute size, plays a determinant role; the extent of the division of labour is positively correlated with a population's size.

This is, of course, an abbreviated rendering of an argument which at one point Durkheim compresses even further in an italicized statement:

The division of labour varies directly with the volume and the density of societies, and if it continues to advance in the course of social development it is because societies regularly become more dense and generally larger.

And he adds:

We are saying, not that the growth and the increasing density of societies *allow*, but that they *necessitate* a greater division of labour. They are not, for the latter, an instrument of its realization, but rather the determinant cause of it. (D 244; 205)

An Argument about 'Representations'

So far, my account of *Division* has emphasized what I consider its main argument: the construct of two basic types of society, each grounded on a different ecological arrangement, and the closely related, *méchaniste* rendering of the process which typically leads from one to the other. By the same token, my account has downplayed one recurrent aspect of the same argument: Durkheim's references to those mentally entertained, subjectively significant 'ways of acting and thinking' which, as we have seen, only two years later, *Règles* was to propose as the 'social facts' *par excellence*.

In *Division* itself, as in other writings, that aspect is mostly encoded in multiple usages of two expressions: 'representation', and 'consciousness' (in the singular or, more often, the plural form). Of these two, the first is probably more significant; 'consciousness' itself is construed as the ensemble of representations harboured at a given time in a mind—an *individual*'s mind, unavoidably! (D 342; 287)—and thus its concept presupposes the other. The 'collective consciousness', for instance, is the set of those representations that are to be found in the minds of *all* the individual members of a given population.

The concept of 'collective consciousness' intervenes at various significant points in *Division*. I will mention three, all connected to the question: what is the role played within 'the representational life' (D 269; 227) of a given society by universally held representations?

First, that role is critical in Durkheim's discussion of a theme of *Division* which we will consider in a later chapter: the prevalence of one or the other kind of law, repressive versus restitutive, as an indicator of its dominant mode of solidarity, respectively mechanical or organic. Essentially, if collective representations are highly dominant in a society's representational life, mechanical solidarity will characterize it, and that society will be sanctioned chiefly by repressive law (typically, criminal law) : if collective representations are a recessive element, organic solidarity will prevail, and will be sanctioned chiefly by restitutive law (typically, the law of contract).

Second, Durkheim also formulates in closely similar terms one of his most pointed criticisms of utilitarian social theory, and of other forms of individualistic theorizing. These presuppose, at the beginning of all social processes, competing individuals endowed with distinctive interests and capacities. However, such individuals only emerge relatively late in the course of social evolution. In fact, one can speak of individuals as relatively self-standing, self-activating entities only to the extent that within the universe of representations lodged within an individual's mind, again, those shared with all other members of the same society have lost significance, relative to those which are instead idiosyncratic to that given individual, since they arise from and affect experiences peculiar to him/her.

Finally, after describing the process of transition from one of society to another chiefly in those 'ecological' terms I have recapitulated above, Durkheim argues that the process involves not only the relative loss of significance of the collective consciousness but also its diminishing 'determinacy'. The description of the contents of *Division*, chapter 3 of book ii given in the table of contents both summarizes the argument I have just given and formulates a further one:

The division of labour cannot progress unless individual variability grows, which cannot occur unless the common consciousness regresses. We have established that this regression takes place. What are its causes?

I. As the social context grows in size, the collective consciousness distances itself from concrete matters and becomes more abstract. Facts to this effect: the (growing) transcendence of the idea of God: the more rational nature of law, of morals, of civilization in general. Such loss of determinacy [*Cette indétermination*] leaves more room to individual variability.

II. The diminishing hold of the segmental arrangement [*type segmentaire*] loosening the individual's tie to his/her context of birth shelters him/her from the action of the elders and thus diminishes the authority of tradition.

III. As the segmental arrangement loses its hold, society less and less envelops the individual, and can thus only to a decreasing extent keep alternative tendencies from emerging. (*D* 413; my translation)

If there are all these indications that the central role attributed by *Règles* to representations is not without precedent in *Division*, why has my restatement of the book's argument in this chapter emphasized instead the ecological arrangements and their dynamic? Why not *give equal time* to representations?

My answer would be: Durkheim himself does not do this. His discussion of 'the progressive loss of determinacy of collective consciousness and its causes' comes within a chapter entitled 'Secondary Factors' (of the division of labour). Also, the few passages in the book where Durkheim poses the question of causal priority between the two orders of phenomena suggest to me a preference for what one may call the material over the mental ones. I will cite one passage, where Durkheim criticizes one of his former teachers at the École Normale:

Mr. Fustel de Coulanges has discovered that the primitive organisation of societies was based on the family and that, in turn, the constitution of the primitive family was grounded on religion. Only, he mistook the cause for the effect. Having once posited the religious conception, without deriving it from anything, he deduced from it the social arrangements he was observing; whereas on the contrary it is these latter ones that account for the force and the content of the religious idea. Given that all those social masses were homogeneous, that is given that the collective type was highly developed and the individual types most rudimentary, unavoidably the psychical life of society took on a religious character. (D 154; *130*)

This validates, I feel, the position I have taken at the beginning of this chapter: *Division* is the key exhibit for the argument that Durkheim was not entirely and always, as I have put it, 'tender-minded'. There is something of a *querelle*, in the contemporary secondary literature,[4] over the question whether the 'tough-minded' Durkheim—evidenced, I suggested, by *Division*'s prevalently ecological strategy both in characterizing the fundamental social types and in accounting for the transition between the one and the other— disappeared in the later writings. As I have already said, it seems to me that the tough-minded Durkheim re-emerges in unexpected places, including his final masterpiece, *Les Formes élémentaires de la vie religieuse*, which on other accounts appears distinctively tender-minded. Perhaps, after *Division*, rather than disappearing, the tough-minded Durkheim does not so much disappear as become recessive. As far as *Division* is concerned, however, the tough and the tender components of his mind-set are not on the same plane. The priority belongs to the former, and a due appreciation of this fact can contribute to a more correct understanding of the complexity and diversity of his life-work, and thus of his theoretical legacy.

Provisional Conclusions Concerning De la division du travail social

This chapter has dealt exclusively with Durkheim's first master-piece, but it has not done justice to all its riches. Later chapters, discussing his conception of modern society and his views on law and on political matters, will return to parts of the text (including the preface to the second edition) to which I have paid little attention so far. I would contend, however, that what I have said so far addresses the book's core argument, and suggests that it is both highly significant and somewhat problematical.

That argument is centred on one of the most sophisticated among the numerous dichotomies developed by great social theorists to grasp conceptually the main varieties of societal organization:[5] in this case, the contrasting constructs of the segmental society characterized by mechanical integration on the one hand and the differentiated society characterized by organic integration on the other. As we have seen, Durkheim used those constructs not only as pointers to the rich variety of socio-historical experience but also as the two ends of a process of development which, under certain conditions (to do with the basic concern of an ecological approach, the population/territory relationship), would lead from one end to the other. Furthermore, he saw this process—structural differentiation, that is, the greater and greater extent to which, within a given society, distinctive ensembles of rules and resources were matched to distinctive social functions—as one that did not stop once the segmental arrangement had been left behind, but continued to produce more and more complex, internally articulated societies.

Durkheim was by no means the first to theorize in this fashion both how diverse human societies can be and have been and what dynamic has led some of them to travel, as it were, from one end of the diversity to the other. Although there were other significant precedents, some of them possibly unknown to Durkheim himself—for instance, the early theories of modernization put forward by Adam Ferguson and John Millar, two Scottish contemporaries of Adam Smith, probably unknown to Durkheim—Spencer was probably the most significant source for this insight of Durkheim's. But Durkheim did not acknowledge this precedent as openly as he might have, for he was too keen to emphasize how differently he interpreted those facts of the matter he shared with, and to some extent he had derived from, Spencer himself, and the divergence between the pragmatic implications of Spencer's and his own interpretations.

As Talcott Parsons was to emphasize,[6] the main twist in Durkheim's version of the differentiation theory of social change was that according to him the differentiation process itself had to be accompanied, and to some extent counterbalanced, by the development of new forms of integration between a society's differentiated parts. He encoded this view in his reiterated statements to the effect that those parts, exactly to the extent that they were differentiated from one another (which meant, to some extent, autonomous of one another), also became mutually dependent, just as the increasingly differentiated parts of a complex biological entity become, by the same token, *organs* with respect to one another and with respect to that entity as a whole. But in spite of his frequent use and occasional abuse of biological analogies, Durkheim was not willing to entrust the realization of the new form of integration—'organic solidarity', as he called it—to the utter spontaneity of the evolutionary process. Hence his emphasis on the necessity of express, self-conscious, authoritatively elaborated and sanctioned mechanisms of regulation—again in the teeth of Spencer's abhorrence for exactly such mechanisms. (I will return to this topic in later chapters.)

I have already expressed my main reservation concerning the contrast between segmental and other societies. There probably have been many human societies where the division of labour was nearly nonexistent: but we just do not know enough about them, for only the breakthrough in some of them of the division of labour, associated with the beginning of relatively advanced technology and of the accumulation of a surplus, would allow them to leave behind traces of their existence sufficient to inform us *how* they existed, let alone how their members thought and felt. On the other hand, all the societies we know something (and sometimes much) about were and are post-segmental.

Thus, one of the two ecological arrangements devised by Durkheim refers to an empty, or nearly empty, set; and the other is *too* full, for it includes exemplars as different as ancient Egypt, a Germanic tribe in Tacitus' time, Rome in republican times, medieval England, the Sun King's France, and contemporary European society. There is nothing wrong with this, except that it diminishes the conceptual purchase which the second construct can have on *any* of those societies, and in particular its bearing on the modernization process.

In spite of this, Durkheim's construction of the differentiation process, including its distinctive concern with integration, has inspired much contemporary theorizing on social change, especially in both the structural/functional (Parsons, Smelser) and in the functional/structural (Luhmann) mode. For that very reason, it has been subjected to much criticism, for instance that voiced by Tilly, the protagonist of a more expressly historically oriented understanding of modernization, who at one point chose to speak of 'useless Durkheim'.[7] On the other hand, in a rightly celebrated reconstruction of modernization itself, centred around the concept of capitalism and very much at odds with structural/functionalism,[8] Anthony Giddens found much use for Durkheim and in particular for his *Division* — more use, may I say, that I would myself, for the reasons I have just suggested.

4

Deviance

The Key Text: Suicide

Le Suicide: Étude de sociologie (1897) is probably Durkheim's best-known work, on various counts.[1] The phenomenon it addresses remains the object of both scholarly and public concern in contemporary societies, and many of the insights he provided into its social causes still sound valid, or at any rate illuminating. Furthermore, *Suicide* articulates most clearly a concept, that of *anomie* (literally 'normlessness'), which not only has had a long and fortunate career within sociology but has repeatedly inspired significant public diagnoses of the contemporary social condition.[2] Finally, it remains today an admirable exemplar of sustained social research, empirically grounded and theoretically oriented, although of course the statistical and other information on the suicide phenomenon accumulated in the century since *Suicide*'s publication dwarfs what we would call today the 'database' constructed with heroic effort by Durkheim himself, and although the modes of analysis he pioneered to examine those data appear today inadequate and sometimes misleading.[3]

On all these counts, *Suicide* has become the referent of a massive tradition of discourse, at the centre of which stand the aspects of the work mentioned above. My own reading of it largely bypasses those aspects to focus on a theme of more general significance for Durkheim and for social theory in general—the nature of normative experience. That is, it is chiefly concerned with the fact that, according to Durkheim, the conduct of individuals is necessarily and materially oriented by norms, by sets of expectations which society sets upon those individuals and sanctions.

Manners of Acting and Thinking

Règles, as we have seen, had conceptualized two central types of 'social fact': *manières d'agir* and *manières de penser*—socially pre-scribed modes, respectively, of acting and of thinking. In *Suicide*, as in much of Durkheim's other work, the centre of attention is held by the former: modes of thinking come into the foreground much later, and do so most creatively in the essay on 'primitive forms of classifi-cation' which he published with Marcel Mauss in 1901–2[4] and in *Formes élémentaires de la vie religieuse*. However, both types of *manières* are made necessary by the same generic fact about human beings: neither their modes of activity nor their perceptions of reality are exclusively grounded on the biological equipment bequeathed to the human species by the course of evolution, and to single human individuals by their ancestors. Far from it: compared with other animals, even those closer to them on the evolutionary scale, humans' ways of acting and thinking are to a very limited extent programmed by instincts and transmitted by genes. Single individuals, instead, apprehend them chiefly from *outside* (to return to the spatial imagery of *Règles*). What they encounter outside themselves are chiefly their fellow humans—or, rather, a distinctive and authoritative social entity, a collectivity made up by those fellow humans, which as we have seen marks with its sanction those ways of acting and thinking it wants its members to acquire and to follow in their acting and thinking.

The human species is a single one, although differentiated into genetically distinctive groupings. Also, its biological design has remained fixed for a very long time, having not varied significantly since the earliest manifestations of human life of which we are aware. Yet human populations are most varied in the ways, in the past and in the present, they normatively and cognitively orient the existence and the experience of their members. This variety, again, witnesses and expresses the looseness, the contingent nature of the relation between the constraints and potentialities bestowed on humans by nature and those which human collectivities construct for themselves and share out to their members.

To phrase this elementary point in contemporary social science language, humans are *cultural* animals through and through. Both *manières d'agir* and *manières de penser* are components of culture so understood—although as far as I am aware it is only in two passages (D 257, 297; 215, 251) that Durkheim uses the term 'culture' in this sense, to designate the totality of socially produced and transmitted arrangements, artefacts, designs for living, characteristic of a human group. Both, furthermore, have in common a fact of which Talcott Parsons made much in his *The Structure of Social Action*[5]—a work based, among other things, on a profound and original reconsideration of Durkheim's work. They operate only through subjective mediation, that is, are capable of being realized in action and in thought only through the individual engaging him/herself (however unselfconsciously) in their realization. Put otherwise, in principle manners of acting do not act themselves through individuals but must be acted upon by them. A contemporary of Durkheim's, Georges Sorel, exressed (as it seems to me) this point in his 'Letter to Daniel Halévy':

We must abandon the idea that the soul can be compared to something moving, which, obeying a more or less mechanical law, is impelled in the direction of certain given motive forces. To say that we are acting implies that we are creating an imaginary world placed ahead of the present world and composed of movements which depend entirely on us. In this way our freedom becomes perfectly intelligible.[6]

Similarly, manners of thinking do not think themselves through individuals without being to some extent embraced, adopted, made sense of.

Durkheim makes this point in the following lengthy quote from *Suicide*, where he criticizes Gabriel Tarde for having placed excessive weight, in his understanding of social phenomena in general, and of suicide in particular, on the operation of what he called 'the instinct of imitation':

When we adopt a fashion or follow a custom, we do what others have done and do every day. However ... this repetition is not due to what we call the instinct of imitation but, on the one hand, to the sympathetic feeling which induces us not to offend the sentiments of our fellows in order better to enjoy our continuing relations with them, on the other to the respect inspired in us by collective ways of acting and thinking and to the pressure exercised upon us by the collectivity in order to prevent dissensions and cultivate in us this sentiment of respect ... Even when we, instead of following usages, rebel against them, the same mode of determination applies; if we adopt a new idea, an unprecedented practice, it is because it possesses intrinsic qualities which make it appear to us as deserving of being adopted . . . In both cases, between the representation of the act and the carrying out of it there intervenes an intellectual operation, which consists in the clear or confused, rapid or slow, appreciation of the determining nature, whatever that may be. [*NB: the translation is uncertain, but so is the text, which is perhaps faulty in the original.*] The manner in which we conform with the mores or the fashions of our country has thus nothing in common with the mechanical, monkey-like imitation on whose account we sometimes reproduce movements which we have witnessed. Between these two ways of acting there is the whole distance which separates reasonable and deliberate conduct from the automatic reflex. The former has its own reasons, even when these are not expressed in the form of explicit judgements. The latter has no such reasons: it originates immediately from the sole sight of the act, without any further mental intermediation. (*S* 112–13; *127–8*).

In this passage Durkheim refers explicitly only to ways of *acting*, and it is not clear whether and how something similar might be said concerning ways of *thinking*. But in *Suicide*, as I have already suggested, it is the former that are the central concern, not the latter; and my own treatment below reflects this preference. In other words, we are interested in the process whereby an individual's action conforms or does not conform to an expectation laid upon it by the group. The last sentence quoted suggests that the process is a minded one, that—as I have already put it—it involves a subjective mediation: an appreciation, however confused, of the expectation in question, a judgement, however rapid, about its validity or suitability.

An implication of this fact, to which I shall return in a later chapter, is that it is at bottom a contingent question whether, for a given individual in given circumstances, the expectation in question will or will not be realized. That is, the existence of the expectation does not, in and of itself, settle the question whether the conduct of individuals will in fact match it. That, so to speak, *depends*. In fact, there are reasons for thinking that, at least in some circumstances, the expectation will fail to induce the individual to behave according to it.

Durkheim had already expressed this position in a chapter of *Règles* where he had argued, sharply and shockingly, that 'crime is normal'. That is, even the strongest expectations laid upon individuals by a society, the norms enjoining individuals to respect the society's most salient interests—such as the life and the bodily integrity of its members, the integrity of the state's institutions—are bound to be violated, to some extent or other, with this or that frequency, by this or by that individual. The very existence of criminal law proves this, for it rests on the assumption that those norms *will* to some extent be infringed, and makes routine arrangements concerning the societal response to such a contingency—a response which inflicts punishment on the violators, and thereby expresses the outrage generated in society by the violation and reasserts the violated norm.

Suicide as Deviance

Suicide deepens and amplifies this argument. First, it goes well beyond a conceptual argument to the effect that 'norms shall be violated', and seeks to determine *under what conditions* this is likely to be the case. (This search, as I indicated, engaged Durkheim in a formidable effort to accumulate and analyse statistical data.) Second, it focuses on the violation of a norm generally not protected by criminal law: the prohibition or at any rate the social disapproval of self-killing (expressed in the moral principles of most religions and in the mores of most known societies). In this manner, *Suicide* points toward a concept related to, but much broader than, that of crime—what today we call deviance or deviant behaviour. It does so, one might say, somewhat timidly, for in our own time most discussions of that concept have embraced a much broader spectrum of counter-normative conduct, ranging from stuttering or obesity to drunkenness and various kinds of mental disorder. In particular, it is somewhat odd that, in *Suicide*, Durkheim fails to conceptualize mental disorder itself as a form of violation of collective norms, generated and patterned to a significant extent by identifiable social circumstances. Instead, in keeping with the views prevailing in his own time, he is content to consider it chiefly as an occurrence grounded in the individual's organic constitution, objectively verifiable without reference to social processes of definition and handling.

Thirdly, *Suicide* marks a further significant advance over *Règles*, in that it analyses empirically a particular form of deviance—suicide itself—in order to identify not just the conditions under which it occurs and some of the related social processes but also some very general societal interests which the prohibition of suicide indirectly expresses. Furthermore, this analytical process leads both to a powerful theoretical critique of modern society and to an express, articulated proposal for its institutional reform.

Before trying to expound the substance (as I see it) of these arguments, let me comment briefly on the method Durkheim follows in developing them. He places those arguments on very sound empirical grounds by addressing his discourse not to the genesis and modalities of individual episodes of suicide (this would amount to 'doing psychology', the last thing he wanted) but to the explanation of suicide *rates*. Each rate is a statistic indicating the incidence of suicide episodes for a given population—not necessarily a national population, but quite as often a population that is a subset of a national one, a subset identified, say, by its occupation, or by its religion—over a certain period of time (generally a year). The suicide rate is generally expressed as the number of suicides per thousand or per hundred thousand members of the population in question. Durkheim presents a huge and painstakingly assembled collection of such statistical data, which reveals two striking features.

First, the suicide rate differs, sometimes very widely, from one population to another (for instance, it is everywhere much larger among city than among country residents). Second, it is basically constant over time (or its variations reveal significant long-term regularities). These two features, Durkheim never tires of telling his readers, indicate that, regardless of the particular circumstances under which an individual member of it commits suicide, each population has, so to speak, a statistically identifiable propensity to suicide of its own. Put another way: on the one hand, each suicide *episode* is an individual story, which calls for a psychologically oriented account of the specific circumstances of its occurrence. Each suicide *rate*, on the other hand, is a collective feature of a given population, and as such, according to the principles stated in *Règles*, should be accounted for sociologically, with reference to other properties of the same population.

The Construction of Suicide Types

However, if the whole argument is placed, as I have suggested, on sound empirical ground, it is not—as it were—built from that ground up. Durkheim is keen to establish that there are sociologically significant *qualitative* differences between suicide rates, that even if two populations present the same suicide rate, the social makings of it may differ between those two populations. But he does not seek to identify those makings inductively; the causes characterizing the three types of suicide Durkheim is keen to differentiate (we shall consider them later) are *posited* by him, not derived empirically. Faced with his huge assembly of suicide rates, distributed among tens and tens of carefully constructed statistical tables, and impatient to subsume that wealth of raw information under a few types, Durkheim reasons that the significantly different causes of suicide reflected in the rates cannot be more than three (four at most), and constructs those, basically, on theoretical grounds (which I consider below). He then seeks the evidence for that reasoning in the data—and, of course, finds it there.

It is perhaps worthwhile to digress a while and retrace the argument in which this critical move is made, in the first chapter of book ii of *Suicide*. At the beginning, Durkheim summarizes the results obtained in book i, which constitutes the *pars destruens* of his argument; that is, it establishes that the 'tendency to suicide' specific to each social group (and revealed by its suicide rate) cannot be explained by reference either to variables relating to the 'organic-psychical constitution of individuals' or to the physical (or, as Durkheim generally calls it, 'cosmic') environment of each group (S 139; *145*).

He then expresses his feeling that the suicide rates themselves are composite data which probably conceal a variety of social tendencies; if so, these ought to be conceptually distinguished from and contrasted with one another in order to interpret the suicide phenomenon as a whole. In other terms, one should distribute the different components of the raw rates into different types, in order to determine the causes and the import specific to each type.

How, then, to constitute those types? One might like to differentiate between suicide episodes in 'morphological' terms, that is, with reference to the account given of each of them as concerns 'the psychical condition in which the person in question found him/herself at the moment of decision, how he/she had prepared to carry it out, how he/she had finally done so, whether he/she was agitated or depressed, calm or eager, anxious or vexed, etc.' (S 140; *146*). However, the information relating to these morphological aspects of the suicide episode is generally either nonexistent or unreliable: 'given the way in which most suicides take place, the observations one would need to have are practically impossible' (S 141; *146*).

Here comes the crucial passage:

However, we can attain our goal via a different avenue. In fact, there can only be different types of suicide in so far as the causes on which they depend are themselves different. [*Says who? one might wonder.*] On this account, we can constitute the social types of suicide not by classifying them with reference to the features indicated previously, but by classifying the causes which engender them ... Without seeking to determine why they differ from one another, we will immediately seek on what social conditions they depend; we will then classify those conditions, according to their similarities and differences, into a certain number of distinct classes, and at this point we can feel assured that to each of these classes there corresponds a determinate type of suicide. In one word, our classification, instead of being morphological, will be, from the beginning, aetiological. (*S* 141; *146–7*)

One senses from the wording that Durkheim is proudly aware that this is a bold move and at the same time uneasily aware that there is something rum about it: 'This method, it is true, has the defect of postulating the diversity of the types without attaining them directly' (142; *147*). But he does not seem to realize that (as I see the matter) there is something arbitrary in his claiming without further ado, as it were, the commanding heights of causal interpretation. Furthermore, much later in the text he appears to have forgotten that *his* suicide types had been postulated rather than established empirically. The opening sentence of the concluding chapter of book ii (the *pars construens* of his whole argument, where Durkheim, so to speak, does his own number) states: 'A finding has now emerged from our research; that is, there is not *a* suicide, but there are suicides' (*S* 312; *277*). As if he had not made plain, at the beginning of that book, that he was fashioning his types out of whole cloth!

The odd thing is that this chapter goes on to derive deductively the morphological features of suicide episodes associated with each type:

One can be sure, then, that there are several kinds of suicide, each qualitatively distinct from the others. But it is not enough to have demonstrated that such differences must exist; one would like to grasp them through direct observation and to know in what they consist. One would like to see the features of the particular suicides group themselves, too, into different classes, corresponding to the types we have already distinguished. In this manner, one would follow the diversity of suicidogenic currents from their social origins down to their individual manifestations.

This morphological classification, which was not possible at the beginning of this study, can be attempted now that it can be grounded on an aetiological classification. (*S* 312; *277*)

I suggest there is something rather cavalier about this way of proceeding. Fortunately, between the two passages from which I have quoted at some length, one at the beginning, the other at the end of book ii, there lies a very strong empirical argument (for all the limitations, as I have suggested, of Durkheim's database, and the weaknesses of his analytical procedures). In any case, the critical remarks I have just made suggest that, at bottom, *Suicide*'s whole argument was more theory-driven, as one would say today, than either Durkheim's own explicit methodological tenets or the broadly positivistic temper of his time would allow him to acknowledge. But this is almost a positive feature of the work in question, when one is—as I am—chiefly interested in the theoretical inspiration behind (or ahead of?) the empirical exercise, and particularly in what *Suicide* has to say about the nature of normative experience.

Why Deviance?

As I have suggested, *Suicide* is a study of deviance; accordingly, most of what it has to say about that topic concerns the reasons why sometimes norms in general, and the norm forbidding individuals to take their own lives in particular, fail to realize themselves in action—in which case they can be reasserted, as we have seen, through the punishment (or, in the case of suicide, the symbolic condemnation) of those violating them.

What are those reasons? The central argument of *Suicide* is all about them; it is complex, and it directly concerns, of course, *only* those reasons which affect the suicide phenomenon. However, it develops a theory of considerable generality about the social genesis of deviance, which I would like to reconstruct below.

The basic insights, as I read them, are three, but they are closely related, almost overlapping. In the first place, some deviance will unavoidably occur because society has diverse and contrasting needs of its own, and on this account it imposes on individuals diverse and contrasting claims, which cannot all be satisfied by the same individuals to the same extent at the same time.

The best statement to this effect (in my judgement) occurs rather late in the book, after Durkheim has developed his argument about three types of suicide, named respectively egoistic, altruistic, and anomic (the terms will be clarified below):

There is no moral ideal which does not combine, in proportions that vary from society to society, egoism, altruism, and a certain measure of anomie. For social life presupposes at the same time that the individual has a certain personality, that he is ready, if society requires, to sacrifice it, finally that he is open, to a certain extent, to ideas of progress. This is why there is not a people in which these three currents of opinion do not coexist, turning man toward divergent and even contradictory directions. Where they temper each other, the moral agent is in a state of equilibrium which shelters him/her from any thought of suicide. But let one of them go past a certain degree of intensity to the disadvantage of the others, and, for the reasons we have seen, it becomes suicidogenic by becoming individualized. (S 363; 321)

To phrase the first insight simply, deviance will occur because of normative pluralism. Since 'it takes a heap o' norms to make a society', sometimes those norms will be difficult to balance against one another in an individual's conduct. Thus the compliance with some will involve (some degree of) deviance from others.

The second insight is to the effect that, for any given norm, there are two ways of deviating from it: by excess or by default—you either overdo it or underdo it. Both things may occur (though not at the same time for the same individual) perhaps again because of normative pluralism: it is the pressure from one norm, the strong loyalty to it, that causes an individual to short-change another norm. (With any luck, come to think of it, a chap may at the same time do that and long-change the norm to which he is particularly loyal!)

In *Suicide*, Durkheim adopts this line of reasoning to conceptualize the three main types of suicide (with a fourth one thrown in, as we shall see). Already in *Division* he had suggested that society can be considered under two chief, compatible aspects:

Under the former, what we mean by society is a more or less organized set of beliefs and sentiments common to all members of the group . . . In the second case, the society . . . is a system of different and specialized functions brought together into definite relationships. These two societies, however, are but one. These are the two faces of the same unified reality, which in spite of that require to be distinguished. (D 99; 83)

This dualism of perspectives, I suggest, persists in modified form in *Suicide*: 'Society is not just an object that attracts to itself, with unequal intensity, the sentiments and the activity of individuals. It is also a power which regulates them [*un pouvoir qui les règle*]' (S 264; 241). Under the first aspect, a society (or other group) possesses more or less 'cohesion'; under the second, it regulates conduct. However, both the 'cohering' and the 'regulating' can occur to an excessive or to an inadequate extent. When a society is too cohesive it tends to generate high rates of altruistic suicide; when it is too little so, it will generate high rates of egoistic suicide. When the society regulates too little, anomic suicide will result; when it regulates to excess, this may lead to a type of suicide, 'fatalistic', which Durkheim mentions only in a footnote (S 311, n.1; 276, $n.$ 25).[7]

A somewhat more detailed discussion of the three major types can be given by developing what I consider Durkheim's third major insight into the genesis of deviance (including suicide). That is: the moral structure of a society is differentiated, for its various moral principles and the related norms are not homogeneously present across social space and social time, but tend to locate themselves preferentially in this or that aspect or phase of social life; some of them are instanced more strongly in some of the groups making up a society, and others in other groups. Where a particular norm is entertained to a particularly strong extent, there its observance is likely to be overdone by at least some individuals, inducing them to deviant acts.

This point is made again and again by Durkheim in *Suicide* (and occasionally elsewhere). The following is one of the most incisive wordings of it, from the last chapter: 'A given moral constitution corresponds with each type of suicide and is connected with it. The one cannot exist without the other; for suicide is merely the form which each moral constitution acquires under particular circumstances, which however cannot but occur' (S 417; 364).

In sum, to put it metaphorically, the moral coat a society wears is a multicoloured one. And this diversification tends to match that attained by its division of labour, for if a society's different parts are to render it their different services, each part must not only instruct its components in specific bodies of knowledge, not only assign to them a specific set of material resources, but also orient them to specific expectations of a moral nature, to the cultivation of specific virtues. Thereby, it exposes them also to the moral risk of specific forms of deviance, implicit in a sense in those very virtues. For suicide itself (one of those forms) is, Durkheim asserts, 'a close relative of veritable virtues of which it constitutes simply an exaggeration' (S 425; 371).

In book ii of *Suicide* (its central part, though in my view many secondary readings have failed to recognize the theoretical riches of the other parts), Durkheim reconnoitres the variety of moral environments presented by societies past and future, both if we compare them to one another and if we analyse each into its distinct components. Thus, he distinguishes between 'primitive' and modern societies (concentrating on these, and particularly on those of Western Europe, because only there his reconnaissance can rest on statistical information), between various societies of the second kind, between groupings within individual societies, and finally between phases and moments in the development of modern societies.

In surveying this variety, on the other hand, he makes analytical use of his (on his own admission) 'postulated' types of suicide. Each of these, Durkheim argues, reflects the prevalence within a given context (a country or a grouping within a country's population) of a distinctive normative complex, which indirectly and (almost always) unintendedly generates a collective tendency to suicide of varying force. This tendency gives notice of itself in the suicide rate characteristic of that context, which is (as we have seen) generally rather stable. Of course, that rate summarizes many highly personal 'roads to suicide', each reflecting idiosyncratic circumstances and vicissitudes. But what is of interest to Durkheim is, even more than the varying magnitude of the suicidal tendency, its varying social nature, which according to him expresses, once more, the context's specific moral environment.

Egoistic Suicide

It is here that his tripartition egoistic/altruistic/anomic suicide comes into play. Durkheim formulates it repeatedly, and at length. I have already suggested that it can be best understood starting from his notion that each society needs to place upon individuals, to a greater or lesser extent, three contrasting moral demands:

Social life presupposes at the same time that the individual has a certain personality, that he is ready, if society requires, to sacrifice it, finally that he is open, to a certain extent, to ideas of progress. (S 363; 321)

'Egoistic suicide' is characteristic of contexts where the first demand is in the foreground. Here, the moral temper (which of course expresses itself though the institutional apparatus of society, its distinctive arrangements concerning the relations between the genders, the production and distribution of wealth, the raising of children, the control over physical violence, and so forth) puts a premium on the individuals' ability to take charge of their own existence, to develop, invest, and risk their own personal resources, to operate each as a self-activating, self-regarding centre of autonomous action and initiative. But this cannot happen without individuals, by the same token, loosening and lengthening their bonds with one another, becoming less aware of the others' interests, less willing and able to entrust their own interests to them, less likely to interact with others in a sustained and intensive fashion. Unavoidably, the contexts within which individuals so disposed interact become less cohesive and coherent, lay less frequent and relevant claims on them, lose significance as sources of inspiration, guidance, and regulation for their activities.

Now suppose that, for whatever reason, an individual who has this rather loose and distant relationship to his/her associates finds him/herself, for whatever reason, in a situation which induces him to dismay and despair and suggests to him the prospect of self-inflicted death as an escape. He has previously learned not to assign a high priority to the claims of his associates upon him, but to orient his own action primarily to his autonomously formed judgement, to the pursuit of his own personal interests, rather than to the obligations he has toward the group. He is not very likely to feel that he *owes* it to the group (or indeed to the several groups to which he—*ex hypothesi*—distantly and loosely belongs) to resist the appeal of a quick and definitive escape from an existence which has become a painful burden, or from a challenge to which suddenly his resources have become unequal. His associates, on the other hand, are not likely to, so to speak, gather around the individual in question, offering him the support he so needs to survive the crisis. They have learned to respect his autonomy, to engage with him only infrequently and for limited purposes; they may not be much aware of his new circumstances and of the threat they pose to his feeling of worth. They do not have, as it were, a strong claim to his living on.

This situation, Durkheim reasons, maximizes the probability that the temptation for the individual to end it all with a bare bodkin will not be resisted. He labels 'egoistic' the suicide that is likely to result, because it crosses the thin line between the conscience the society has previously imparted to the individual that his/her happiness is a significant social value, the responsibility for which belongs primarily to him/herself (Durkheim calls this 'individualism'), and the sensation that nothing in the world matters except the balance between pleasure and pain, a balance which for that given individual is currently very negative.

The following is one of Durkheim's many eloquent statements of his point, drawn from *Suicide*'s last chapter:

In the societies and in the social contexts where the dignity of the person is the supreme goal of conduct, where man is a God to man, the individual is strongly inclined to take as God the man which he himself is, to turn oneself into an object of his own cult. When morals are chiefly concerned to give him a high notion of himself, a combination of circumstances suffices to render him incapable of perceiving anything above himself. Individualism, undoubtedly, is not necessarily egoism, but is near to it; one cannot foster the one without advancing further the other. It is thus that egoistic suicide emerges (*S* 416; 363–64).

The chapter on 'egoistic suicide' is, of course, full of empirical instantiations of this reasoning. Here, Durkheim produces evidence to the effect that the suicide rate is particularly high in societies and other social settings where the individual is encouraged to attain a maximum of autonomy with respect to groups, and where as a consequence the society as a whole or its component groups have a relatively thin and underdeveloped structure. I shall just give two major examples.

First, Durkheim interprets along the lines suggested above what he considered a soundly established finding concerning the association between religious membership and the incidence of suicide. The finding was that one of the religions present in European societies, Protestantism, presents a much higher suicide rate than Catholicism, and Judaism comes last in this particular regard. Leaving Judaism aside, the comparison between Protestantism and Catholicism is most significant as it concerns the existence and nature of a specifically 'egoistic' suicide. Why?

Protestant confessions attach a much higher value than Catholicism to the self-guided, conscience-grounded relationship between the individual faithful and God and/or the Church. Protestant churches, accordingly, tend to be much more loosely structured than the Catholic Church; they authoritatively impart to their faithful many fewer credences and address to them fewer directives for action, control the interpretation and monitor the realization of those credences and directives to a lesser extent, involve the believers in less frequent and less solemn rituals and other occasions for interacting on a communal basis and for asserting their affiliation to the Church and their allegiance to its hierarchy (if any).

Thus, Protestant churches may condemn suicide as much as the Catholic Church does; but they constitute a less cohesive, less intensely social environment, more respectful of individual autonomy, less exacting and interfering—but also, by the same token, less supportive of individuals confronted with serious crises; and to some extent this effect extends to the societies and cultures where Protestantism is the prevalent form of religion. Here, as a consequence, the suicide rate is high, relative to that for Catholics or for prevalently Catholic societies.

Second, the suicide rate is much higher for single (adult) individuals than for spouses, and for spouses without than for spouses with children. As Durkheim phrases it, marriage and a family 'preserve' the spouses and parents from suicide—an effect which, incidentally, is stronger for men than for women. As he interprets this finding, it reflects again the fact that married people, and especially those with children, live out their existence in a very different social environment from single and/or childless people. They are necessarily, though of course to a varying extent, surrounded by a group which has strong claims upon their resources, their energies, their attention, their sentiments—indeed, their existence itself. By the same token, they know where to turn in a crisis; in any case, they have long lived their life on the assumption that it could not be totally self-centred, but always had to justify itself, direct itself, by taking into some account the needs of others. Both this knowledge and the availability of constant and close associates who can bolster up and to some extent reassure and protect the individual at risk makes these individuals less likely to commit a desperate act.

Note that here, as elsewhere in *Suicide*, Durkheim attacks what one may call a utilitarian conception of suicide. According to this conception, the rate of the phenomenon should be higher for people more exposed to pressures, more inconvenienced as it were, more vexed, tried, exhausted by the objective circumstances of their existence, by material limitations in particular. The immunity (relative, of course) from suicide conferred in particular by parenthood, and which is indeed greater for parents of larger families—or for that matter the fact that peasants everywhere have lower suicide rates than people practising physically less burdensome occupations, protected from the vagaries of the weather—is incompatible with that viewpoint, and disproves it.

Altruistic Suicide

The chapter on 'altruistic' suicide discusses two different situations, both of which discourage individuals from attaining and preserving a strong sense that they matter *as individuals*. First, there is a group of societies about whose suicide rates we have no reliable information, but some qualitative evidence concerning occurrences of suicide which are of a very different character from 'egoistic' ones. It is a rather heterogeneous group, for it comprises a number of 'primitive' societies but also some societies of classical antiquity, and societies such as Japan or India which are obviously in no way primitive but which according to Durkheim preserve some archaic traits. Second, the relatively solid statistical information data concerning modern European societies from which Durkheim built his database contain evidence of a type of suicide again different from the 'egoistic' one, localized within highly specific groups.

What these very different social circumstances have in common is a pattern of relations between the individual and the group which Durkheim had already identified in highly 'primitive' (or 'inferior') societies where the division of labour barely exists and whose solidarity, accordingly, is mechanical in nature. Put briefly, the pattern is that in these societies individuals do not (yet) exist, except as separate bodies; for the great majority of the representations which people the minds of the society's members, which construe the reality around them, and upon which they act are shared by one and all. As we have already seen, many of those representations are typically vivid, strong, and cogent, discourage individuals from developing variants of and deviations from them, and are protected from such variants and deviations by the threat of collective displeasure, manifested as punishment.

In these circumstances, the group to which individuals belong represents not only the sole source of their identity, of their sense of worth, but also the dominant target of their preoccupations, their efforts, their desires. Its survival, its welfare, its power in the world beyond it constitute a commanding concern, which transcends all mundane ones, relating only to each individual's wellbeing. All that the individual has and is belongs to the group; in comparison with that, he/she is an insignificant entity, which assigns little moral importance to faculties, cares, experiences exclusive to him or herself.

Thus downgraded, individuals are open to two compatible

feelings: one, that the only way to justify their own existence is to devote all their energies, and if necessary to sacrifice that existence itself, to the welfare of the group; two, that they themselves, their private sufferings or their joys, have no significance in the broader scheme of things, that they are dispensable, and their very survival is a morally indifferent matter.

To these feelings correspond two fairly different variants of 'altruistic suicide': one where the suicidal act takes place in compliance with the group's express or implied expectation that the individual should surrender his/her life in order to assert the superiority of the group and advance its interests; and one where the suicidal act flows from the individual's particularly diminished sense of his/her own worth and significance. The contrast with egoistic suicide is particularly marked in the first case, to which the label 'altruistic' is particularly appropriate:

We are here confronted with a type of suicide most sharply characterized with respect to the previous [egoistic] one. While that is due to an excess of individuation, this has its cause in a highly deficient individuation. One comes from the fact that the society, disarticulated in this or that particular point or even as a whole, allows the individual to escape it; the other, from the fact that it holds him too tightly under its dependency. Since we have labelled *egoism* the state in which the self [*le moi*] finds itself when it lives its own personal life and obeys only itself, the word *altruism* expresses well the opposite state, that where the self does not belong to itself, where it is confounded with something other than itself, where the polestar of its conduct is located outside of it, that is, in the group to which it belongs.   (S 238; 221)

In order to apply the conceptual label 'altruism' also to the other type of suicide, Durkheim attaches to this one an additional qualification, and calls it *obligatory* altruistic suicide, distinguishing it from a pattern where society does not so much expect or encourage the suicidal act as permit it or appear indifferent to its occurrence. Thus, a suicide which Durkheim labels 'optional' (*facultatif*) may become a frequent response to situations of distress and unease which may not strike us as particularly dramatic and upsetting; for example, 'we know with what facility the Japanese open up their belly for the most insignificant reason' (S 239; 222). But the broader label 'altruistic' is valid also for these circumstances, for it pinpoints a common underlying cause:

When, from childhood on, one becomes used not to make much of one's existence and to despise those who are too attached to their own, it is inevitable that one dispose of it at the slightest provocation. One can opt without much pain for a sacrifice which has such a low cost. Thus, just as with obligatory suicide, these practices are connected with what is most fundamental in the morals of inferior societies. Since they cannot maintain themselves except when the individual does not have distinct interests of his own, the individual must be trained to renunciation and to total abnegation; from here come these suicides, including spontaneous ones. Just as with those more expressly prescribed by society, they are due to this condition of impersonality or, as we have called it, of altruism, which one may consider as the morality characteristic of primitives. (S 240; 222-3)

But both obligatory and optional suicide, according to Durkheim, give evidence of themselves also in modern societies. Not, however, at large, because these societies, taken as a whole, are characterized if anything by the prevalence of egoistic suicide; rather, within specific social locations, and in particular within the armed forces. These generally reveal suicide rates in excess of those of the larger society, for reasons having to do with the essentially primitive, anti-individualistic nature of their distinctive morality:

The soldier's foremost quality is a kind of impersonality which is nowhere to be found to the same extent within civilian life. He must be trained not to make much of his own person, for he must be ready to sacrifice it as soon as he is ordered to. Even outside of extraordinary circumstances, in peacetime and in the context of the day-to-day experience of the occupation, discipline requires that he obeys without arguing and even, sometimes, without understanding. But this requires a degree of intellectual self-renunciation which is incompatible with individualism. One must have a much diminished sense of one's individuality if one is to comply so submissively with external directives. In one word, for the soldier the principle of his conduct lies outside of himself; and this is the essential feature of the altruistic condition. Of all component parts of our modern societies, the army is that which most recalls the structure of inferior societies. The army, too, constitutes a massive and tightly woven body which holds tightly the individual and prevents him from moving according to motions of his own. (S 254; 234)

But let us not forget that the command that the individual should place his/her very existence at the disposal of the collectivity is but an exaggerated version of a more general demand, indispensable to all society. In turn, especially in circumstances which do not require the supreme sacrifice, a suicide act may be considered a form of exaggerated compliance with that command or the underlying demand.

In the final chapter of *Suicide* Durkheim explores these somewhat paradoxical connections:

Since the strict subordination of the individual to the group is the principle on which [inferior societies] rest, altruistic suicide constitutes, so to speak, an indispensable component [*procédé*] of collective society. If man did not rate his own life as of little consequence, he would not be what he must be, and, given that he does not make much of it, it is inevitable that anything may become a pretext for his surrendering it. There is thus a close link between the practice of such suicide and the moral organisation of those societies. The same holds for those particular settings where abnegation and impersonality are required. But then, the military spirit cannot be strong unless the individual becomes detached from himself, and this detachment necessarily opens the way for suicide. (*S* 416; 363)

Anomic Suicide

So much for two of the very general rules which Durkheim indicates in a statement I will now quote for the third time and for the respective types of suicide:

Social life presupposes at the same time that the individual has a certain personality, that he is ready, if society requires, to sacrifice it, finally that he is open, to a certain extent, to ideas of progress. (*S* 363; 321)

What of the third norm, which leads to 'anomic suicide'? The underlying idea is that, as we have seen, societies are characterized not only by a certain amount of cohesion—or lack of it—but also by a certain amount of regulation—or lack of it. In that statement, this idea is expressed somewhat elliptically, and needs to be expanded somewhat. Societal regulation tends to crystallize the status quo, to impart a certain momentum and a certain inertia to the existent conditions of societies, by locking individuals into certain repetitive patterns of conduct. Such regulation, if it is observed constantly and everywhere over the social space, induces rigidity in the society in question, and puts at risk the very value it seeks to protect—that society's survival—if new circumstances arise which the existing rules do not foresee or do not adequately provide for. To moderate this risk, and allow for the innovations in 'ways of thinking and of acting' those circumstances may require, societal regulation should not be too comprehensive and too tight; it should leave uncovered certain areas and moments of social life, be tempered by some allowance for imaginative, unprecedented variation, for conduct discrepant with respect to routinized proceedings. It is as if the entire body of rules existent in a given situation were complemented by an unspoken, override rule which to an extent tempers and relativizes them—something like 'Don't take rules too seriously' or 'Rules should not/need not be observed by absolutely all the people all the time'.

Once more, this particular rule is liable to be maintained and complied with to an excessive extent; and this, too, generates a societal risk. Society may become too little committed to its normal rules, too little assured of their validity, and as a result many social expectations may become destabilized, lose their legitimacy and effectiveness. Under these conditions, too many people too much of the time may be at a loss as to what to think, do, expect of themselves and of others. The prevailing condition may become one of 'anomie', of normlessness: one where widely agreed, understood, respected standards of conduct no longer exist, or at any rate do not exist for some spheres and phases of social life of considerable general significance.

Why would such a situation produce its own type of suicide, 'anomic', corresponding presumably with a distinctively high suicide rate? The normative fabric of a society is not important only for the collective body; it is also important for the moral guidance it provides individuals. These, in deliberating and assessing their own conduct, refer largely to existing rules; the conformity of their conduct with those rules reassures them as to their own moral worth. By the same token, it is the normative fabric of society that indirectly confers meaning on the individuals' very existence, and in particular allows them to validate, direct, and limit their desires, to invest affect into what they are and have, to set boundaries to their own aspirations, to appreciate and take pride in what they have accomplished, to make sense of the privations, exclusions, and liabilities to which they are exposed by their circumstances.

This ability to place a morally rewarding and sustaining interpretation upon those circumstances, upon one's own biography, one might say, is what is at risk for individuals in a largely or increasingly anomic society, particularly when the strivings inspired in them by the prevailing encouragement towards enterprise, innovation, ambition fail to attain the expected outcomes. Indeed sometimes, even when they do not so fail, the pursuit itself of improvement in one's own condition, rather than the improvements themselves, may become the focus of one's existence. Under these conditions, those strivings may induce in individuals a perpetual tension, an inability to find satisfaction in their achievements.

People move on, restlessly, in a moral vacuum. One can well imagine that, particularly when an individual in these circumstances encounters a crisis, a serious setback, in absolute terms or in relation to what he/she sees happening to others, this situation may induce in him/her a kind of moral giddiness, a 'taste of ashes', a disgust for life and its meaninglessness, that lead in turn to suicide.

Of the empirical arguments Durkheim adduces to substantiate this reasoning, two strike me as particularly significant. One is formulated at the societal level, and asserts (the evidence adduced is perhaps not particularly strong) that suicide rates in contemporary societies are particularly high not only in times of economic bust (when they could be interpreted in utilitarian terms, with reference to the sudden darkening of the social horizon) but also in times of economic boom. This allows Durkheim to argue that 'anomic suicide' is caused by the loss of correspondence between sanctioned social expectations and economic circumstances, and by the resultant emergence of a normative vacuum, which so to speak unbinds the individuals' desires and aspirations, *not* by the objective worsening of those circumstances.

The second argument concerns the particularly high suicide rate associated with divorce. This can be expected to induce a kind of micro-anomie, in that it throws out of gear, for the disrupted couple, the moral framing of desires, the disciplining and moderating of practices and aspirations, normally associated with the married condition. The resultant rise in the suicide rate, incidentally, is particularly marked in the case of men; as husbands particularly benefit from the 'coefficient of preservation from suicide' induced by that condition, so do divorced husbands suffer from the 'aggravation effect' associated with divorce itself.

Once more, the last chapter provides an impressive phrasing of the general point:

Among peoples where progress is and must be rapid, the rules which contain individuals must be sufficiently flexible and changeable; if they maintained the unmoving rigidity which they possess within primitive societies, the evolution they entail could not take place at an adequate speed. However, it is then inevitable that desires and ambitions, less strongly contained, at certain points overflow powerfully. Once one instructs men in the principle that they are duty bound to progress, it is more difficult to turn them toward resignation; as a consequence, the number of discontented and restless people cannot but increase. All morals concerned with progress and improvement are thus inseparable from a certain amount of anomie. (S 416–17; 364)

A Critique of Modern Society

As I have already indicated (and as the passage above may suggest to the reader), Durkheim puts to use the distinction between the three very general norms to which I have repeatedly referred, and the rest of *Suicide*'s argument about the respective suicide types, not just to identify the moral requirements of all societies (and groups) and the related 'deviant' consequences but also to articulate a powerful diagnosis of modern society in particular. This diagnosis is composed of two chief arguments.

The first is to the effect that, as its peculiarly high and rising suicide rates reveal, modern society is currently in an unbalanced, pathological condition, which needs to be soon redressed if worse is to be avoided. This argument is somewhat baffling. Consider that, according to a famous statement in *Règles*, 'crime is normal'—a statement generalizable as 'deviance is normal'. Consider, further, the numerous statements in *Suicide* to the effect that each society has the deviance types and rates consequent upon its distinctive moral structure, and finally the categorical antithesis Durkheim posits (again in *Règles*) between 'normal' and 'pathological'. Yet in *Suicide* it is as if Durkheim were saying, of modern society in particular, 'I know deviance is normal—but this is ridiculous!' We will see below whether and how this apparent contradiction can be reconciled.

The second argument is to the effect that modern society is characterized (to pathological effect) by the convergence and by the particular strength of two of the three general norms I repeatedly mentioned above: those engendering the 'suicidogenic currents' leading respectively to egoistic and to anomic suicide. Even aside from these particular consequences—after all, suicide remains a quantitatively very limited phenomenon, significant chiefly for what it symbolizes—the strong prevalence of those two norms reveals itself, in contemporary industrial societies, through a number of troubling phenomena; in particular, the loss of coherence and cohesion of societies at large and of many of their component groups (see for instance the growing divorce rate), the contentiousness and unruliness of public life and the frequency and intensity of social conflict, the unleashing of individual and collective egoism, the lack of a sense of mutual obligation between individuals, the recurrence of marked and destructive economic crises, the prevalence of a sense of collective melancholia, the sensation of instability and precariousness engendered by the speed of social and cultural change, the inability or unwillingness to subscribe to or construct collective, authoritative arrangements for monitoring and disciplining the social process.

The strong presence and the convergence of egoism and anomie concur in inducing these phenomena. The first is associated with an excessive emphasis on the centrality of the self, on an individualism which degenerates into atomism. That is, each individual judges the world and orients his/her action chiefly if not exclusively by reference to him/herself, orients himself predominantly to his/her own private interests, ignoring what he/she owes to other individuals, and to the collectivity which posits and sustains all individuals but, under contemporary conditions, finds them unresponsive to its own demands. (A similar view has been expressed in our own times under the label of 'narcissism'.) Anomie entails an inability to set enforceable boundaries to the individual's pursuits, a sense that nothing much matters, everything is possible; it destroys those normative frameworks that could at the same time bind and sustain individual existence, and thus threatens it with meaninglessness.

I have expressly employed, in so characterizing *Suicide*'s critical view of modern society, the rhetoric associated with many antimodernist positions, and in particular with the turn-of-the-century forms of critique of mass society; for Durkheim shares some of those positions. But, as I have stated in my first chapter, he dissents from others, in ways which bear also on our topic here.[8]

In the first instance, many critiques of mass society (particularly those to be found among German writers) lay the phenomena they lament chiefly at the door of (as they see them) negative *cultural* developments, such as secularization, the infatuation with reason characteristic of the Enlightenment tradition, or the excessive faith in progress characteristic of nineteenth-century positivism. Durkheim, instead, maintains in *Suicide* a strong sense of the causal priority of *structural* developments. For instance, he dissents strongly from a view that attributes the high incidence of suicide in some Oriental societies to the prevalence of pantheistic views:

One cannot concede that it is pantheism that produced the suicide [rate]. It is not abstract ideas that lead men and one should not account for historical developments by playing upon purely metaphysical concepts. Among people as among individuals, representations serve above all to express a reality not of their own making; on the contrary, they derive from it, and if subsequently they can modify it, this can only happen to a limited extent. Religious conceptions are products of the social context, rather than producing it themselves, and if, once formed, they react upon the causes which had brought them about, this reaction cannot be very profound. Thus, if what constitutes pantheism is a more or less radical denial of all individuality, such a religion can only arise within a society where, in fact, the individual is of no consequence, that is totally lost within the group. For men cannot represent the world to themselves except through the image of the smaller social world in which they live. (S 245; 226–7).

Durkheim applies the same reasoning in accounting for the differences between Protestant and Catholic suicide rates. At first, as we have seen, he emphasizes a distinctive feature of the Protestant belief system, the principle of 'free examination', that is, a commitment to the validity of the individual's personal reading and interpretation of the Scriptures, which ends up loosening the structure of the confessional community. But then he complements and substantially corrects that insight as follows:

Let us attempt to understand correctly this relationship. Free examination is, itself, only the effect of another cause. When it makes its appearance, when men, after having for ages received all their belief ready made from tradition, claim the right to form it themselves, this is not due to the intrinsic attractions of the free search for truth, for this involves as many pains as it does joys. Rather, it is because by now they need that freedom. But that need can only have one cause: the disarray of traditional beliefs . . . If a new system of beliefs had constituted itself which everybody considered above discussion just as the ancient one had been, one would not have thought to discuss the latter. (S 157–8; 158–9)

Durkheim differs from the standard anti-modernist line also in the way he construes the structural developments which characterize modernity and which *for the time being* (I stress this qualification, to be clarified below) generate much of the disorder and dismay of contemporary industrial societies. What is decisive is

the development undergone by economic functions, approximately over the course of the last two centuries. Formerly they played a secondary role, but today they are uppermost . . . On that account one has said of our societies, not without reason, that they are or tend to be essentially industrial. Obviously a form of activity which has acquired such a place within social life at large cannot remain unregulated to such an extent without engendering the deepest dislocations. It becomes the source of a general state of demoralization . . . Thus, the absence of any discipline over economic life can but extend its effects beyond the sphere of the economy itself and bring about a lowering of public morality. (*D* pp. iv–v; pp. *xxxiii–xxxiv*)

In modern societies, then, the institutions and processes of the economic sphere have become central and dominant, and have displaced toward the periphery previously dominant institutions and processes such as religion or politics. It so happens that the economic sphere is by its very nature, at any rate when it has autonomized itself from others, prone to egoism and anomie. Egoism, because its distinctive dynamics depends chiefly on the self-regarding, self-seeking market activities of individuals construed as sovereign, competing entities; anomie, because the competition process itself places a premium on the participants' capacity for innovation, for devaluing existent arrangements, inventing new products, creating new markets.

Furthermore, Durkheim advanced some at least of his criticisms of modern society, particularly in his early work, from a standpoint foreign to most anti-modernist critiques. Convinced as he was that on many counts modernization had represented a significant progress over previous social conditions, and committed as he was in particular to the rights of individuals to freedom and equality, he criticized some social conditions as representing the current society's failure to deliver on the promise of modernity. On some counts, that is, modern society was not modern enough.

For example, a central argument in *Division*, as we have seen, is that the advance of the division of labour promotes the development of a new, organic form of solidarity. But the last book of that work suggests that some existing institutions—such as the right to inherit the possessions of one's parents—or the fact that normally employees are in a position of material inferiority vis-à-vis employers, contrast with that development. More generally, the new forms of law and morality necessary to establish that solidarity are coming too slowly into being. At the very end of *Division*, Durkheim restates this point:

Deep changes have occurred, within a very short time span, in the structure of our societies; they have freed themselves from the segmental type at a rate and to an extent unprecedented in history. As a consequence, the morality corresponding to that social type has retreated, but without the other developing fast enough to fill the ground which the first left within our consciousnesses ... The functions which had become disassociated in the course of the trouble have not had the time to adjust to one another, the novel life which has emerged suddenly has been unable to organize itself completely, and above all in such a manner as to satisfy the need for justice which has become more ardent in our hearts ... What is necessary, is to put an end to this anomie, to find ways of making these organs which currently contrast with one another in their discordant motions cooperate smoothly, to induce into their relations more justice by reducing those external inequalities on which bad conditions [le mal] rest. (D 405; 339–40)

In *Suicide*, published four years after *Division*, Durkheim proposed not so much the reforms needed to bring modern society into equilibrium as an institutional mechanism whereby such reforms could be worked out and applied; he re-presented that argument in the preface to the second edition of *Division*. (We shall consider those proposals in the chapter on political institutions.) However, one might say that over the years that followed Durkheim progressively lost faith not so much in the validity of those proposals as in the likelihood of their being publicly recognized as valid and put in place. This realization introduced into his thinking a vein of pessimism, and perhaps led to an increasingly negative appraisal of the moral significance of modernity.

In Lewis Carroll's *The Hunting of the Snark* , the Butcher finds himself having to explain to the Beaver that $1 + 1 + 1 = 3$. Although it's a tough assignment,

> 'The thing can be done,' said the Butcher, 'I think'.
> 'The thing must be done, I am sure'.
> 'The thing shall be done!'

It is as if Durkheim, when considering modern society, could follow the Butcher through the first two ringing affirmations, but baulked at the third.

5

What *Is* Society for Durkheim?

A Missing Definition

Some commentators have noted an oddity in Durkheim's writings. The expression 'society' recurs in them very frequently and, one might say, strategically; that is, he deploys it emphatically, at the very centre of arguments where he articulates those he considers his most distinctive and strongest positions. One might even say that that he uses 'society' worshipfully: for some of those arguments amount to a hymn to society, enthuse over society's greatness, its power, perfection, benevolence, majesty, its entitlement to the individual's awe and devotion. Yet—and this is the oddity—'society' is an expression Durkheim never defines. He defines a number of closely related ones—in particular, as we have seen in Chapter 2, 'social facts'—but when it comes to 'society' itself he systematically fails to abide by his own recommendation that the referents of scientific arguments be defined explicitly, and as early as possible in the course of inquiry.

This chapter starts out from this simple observation—Durkheim never defines 'society'—in order not so much to suggest how he *might* have defined it, but rather to reflect on a broader question: what *is* society for Durkheim? The answer takes the form of a relatively diffuse argument, some aspects of which are not drawn from Durkheim's writings, but (I would maintain) formulate and develop understandings implicit in them, and particularly in those previous to *Formes élémentaires de la vie religieuse*. The chapter dealing with this work will suggest some ways in which it modifies or qualifies the argument developed here.

A Contingent Reality

What, then, *is* society for Durkheim? I will start with a negative answer, which addresses a frequent misunderstanding of his position, a misreading of his insistence that social facts are real, that they are things and ought to be treated as such. Society is *not* a substance existing in space; studying it is not the same kind of activity as locating, mapping, and describing Mount Everest. It does not have the same kind of reality as individuals have, for each of them *is* a substance, exists in space. Rather, society should be conceived as a process, as a set of events, of activities. It should be thought of as a flow of energy rather than as a stock of objects. Put otherwise, we should not think of it so much as a theatre building or a stage but rather as a theatrical performance. Society is a contingent reality, real *in so far as* certain things go on.

In so far as *what* things go on? One might think of society as the sum total of events occurring between individuals, as the totality of their interactions, of the ways in which they impinge on one another, of their reciprocal exchanges of energy. But this is too wide and comprehensive a view of society, identifies it with too much that goes on. It does not distinguish, so to speak, between noise and signal.

A more plausible approximation to society's reality is the following. Society is not coterminous with that enormous set of events; it stands at some remove from all that buzz and fuss. It is more abstract than that: it exists in so far as *those* events, all those buzzing activities, all those ways individuals affect one another, are withdrawn from randomness, patterned, made to recur in relatively predictable fashion, standardized, rendered uniform across time, space, individuals, circumstances. We might thus identify society itself with those uniformities, see it as the sum total of the patterns affecting the interactions taking place between individuals.

However, this is again too comprehensive an understanding of society. For those interactions are patterned in all manner of ways, some of which are not social in nature. In the first instance, individuals are physical bodies, aggregates of matter endowed with mass and velocity, and affected by those properties also in their interactions with one another. Society has nothing to do with the resultant regularities—those which in a passage of the preface to the second edition of *Règles* Durkheim attributes to 'the rigidity of certain arrangements of molecules'—significant as they may be.

In the second instance, individuals are animals, and as such they are the sites of biological activities, the points of origin of biological processes which affect and pattern their interactions. In the language of his generation, Durkheim sees humans as endowed with instincts, and as controlled by instincts, to some extent, also in the way they relate to one another. Again, the resultant regularities may be empirically very significant (D 311; 262). Yet Durkheim on the whole discounts that significance; in any case, for him biologically grounded patterns of interaction are not among society's constituents. In so far as the relations between human individuals are patterned by the biological needs and resources they possess *qua* animals, you do not (yet) *have* society. Society begins where instincts end.

Two Kinds of Representation

There are two compatible ways of characterizing what begins at that point, what distinctive patterns constitute society. One is to think of them as 'cultural', that is, as originating from human activities which, while grounded in the specific biological properties of humans, are not tightly programmed by them, but vary in space and time much more than those properties do, and accordingly generate hugely diverse patterns.

Durkheim only occasionally uses the expressions 'culture/cultural' in this meaning (for two examples see D 257, 297; 215, 251), though more frequently he implies it in his writings. But his favourite characterization of distinctively social patterns is different, and is signalled in his writings by the recurrent expression 'representation', understood as 'mental image', and by the occasional emphasis on the 'psychical' nature of social reality—as in the bold statement, 'a collective psychology would constitute all of sociology'.[1] Put otherwise, Durkheim conceptualizes society as the set of *minded* patterns affecting the interactions of human individuals. Society exists, for Durkheim, in so far as those interactions are controlled by mental images, rather than by the laws of matter or by instincts.

But this characterization is only a provisional result, requiring some elaboration. 'Mental images' is a somewhat generic term, and Durkheim himself often differentiated it. As we have seen, he spoke of *manières d'agir et de penser*, manners of acting and thinking, as the 'social facts' *par excellence*. But perhaps he did not make enough of this distinction, thinking that both 'manners', *qua* social facts, shared the property of being obligatory, indicated in turn by their being sanctioned. This is somewhat problematical, as indicated for instance by Luhmann's emphasis on the contrast between normative and cognitive expectations.[2]

According to these arguments, the sanction is a conceptual component only of normative expectations. 'Thou shalt not kill' is a *normative* expectation because if we encounter a course of events that does not conform with it we do not abandon it or revise it to match those events, but reassert it in the face of facts by inflicting a penalty on the killer. As Roman jurists had it, 'the law forbids that something be done; but if it should get done, law does not undo it, rather inflicts a punishment on the doer'. As against this, those expectations which, failing their realization in reality, are instead abandoned or revised to match the facts, are *cognitive*.

Durkheim was keen to assert that society authoritatively imparts to individuals not just directives for action, but perspectives on reality, ways to conceive of it. Thus, in *Formes*, he elaborated a sociology of knowledge in sharp contrast both with Descartes's emphasis on the self-standing thinking subject and with Kant's conception of the a priori equipment of the human mind; for Durkheim saw the collectivity as the source of all basic instruments of thought, and signally of the 'categories'.

This may have hindered his recognition that 'manners of thinking', ways of conceiving reality, cannot be made binding on individuals in the same way that manners of acting can. However, he did acknowledge that the rules of conduct which can be derived from them—for instance, how to handle chemical elements which we know to become explosive if allowed to come into contact with one another, or how to apply to damaged tissues a poultice formed from herbs known to have certain healing properties—are of a different nature from institutional rules; the negative effects of their neglect follow automatically, not through the mediation of human agents applying sanctions (*S&P* 59–60; 42–3).

In any case, in his most forceful pronouncements on the nature of social reality (particularly those contained in the *Leçons de sociologie*) Durkheim's emphasis lay chiefly on what he had called previously manners of acting, and later subsumed under the concept of rule, *règle*. This expression clearly refers to rules of conduct, and his understanding of these is probably based on the concept of *regula juris*, juridical rule. 'There ought to be a law' is a banal but appropriate way of conveying much that Durkheim intends when he comments on current states of affairs and prospects a conscious intervention on them. Now, juridical rules are normative expectations *par excellence*, in the sense indicated previously; they assert themselves through sanctions in case of events which fail to conform with them. (On this account I propose to translate Durkheim's *règle* by 'norm' rather than by 'rule'.)

As we have seen in Chapter 2, the emphasis on the sanction serves another, related purpose in Durkheim's argument. Within the ensemble of representations entertained within the minds of individuals, sanctions mark those which are part of society, distinguishing them from those which are private to individuals and thus not part of society. It is not the minded-ness of human activities as such that constitutes society, but a particular kind of minded-ness—that which is oriented to and guided by representations present within individual minds but collective in nature. Society is the sum total of representations of the latter kind; it exists in so far as the interactions of individuals are controlled by institutional rules—or by compelling currents of emotion or opinion that are collective in nature though they have not (yet) crystallized as such rules—rather than by considerations entirely private to themselves.

Durkheim's Pathos

Having taken these steps toward an understanding of what Durkheim meant by society, let us reconsider a point made above: society is a *contingent* reality. I would suggest that although Durkheim never expressly articulated that point, his deepening awareness of it progressively generated in his writings a distinctive note of sombre concern, manifest particularly in his reflections on modern society, which I would like to call Durkheim's *pathos*. For the expression 'contingent' (as I use it here; Durkheim, so far as I know, does not use it) means: something is the case, but it *need not* be. It means: whether something is the case, *depends*. Applied to particular social arrangements, these meanings may suggest liberating insights, such as: the current ways of doing (or of viewing) things are intrinsically arbitrary; they can be improved (or worsened); they can be replaced by alternative ones. But when predicated of something as comprehensive as society itself, 'contingency' is liable to induce some disquiet in anybody but a nihilist—which Durkheim definitely was not.

In what senses, according to the previous argument, can we say that society is a contingent reality? First, it is not a substance, but a process, a performance, an *in so far as* reality. Second, it exists at some remove from the buzzing reality of interactions between individuals, as the sum total of collective representations controlling those interactions. But, third—and this point needs to be more explicit than it has been so far—those representations are not self-enforcing; they need to be acted upon by individuals, and the minds of those individuals contain also other representations, which are not collective, and action upon which has at best an indifferent and at worst a negative effect when it comes to sustaining the reality of society.

Now, collective representations are not, so to speak, helpless in the face of those other representations. As we have seen time and again, norms, which are collective representations *par excellence*, are backed by sanctions, and the awareness of sanctions can typically motivate compliance with norms, through the promise of reward or the threat of punishment. But this, alas, confirms rather than obviates the contingent nature of society. For, as we have also seen, the sanction itself does not depend on the intrinsic nature of the representation, but is attached to it by society itself: nothing but the norm 'thou shalt not kill' ensures that the act of killing will have as a consequence the punishment of the killer. It gets worse: that consequence is not, in fact, 'ensured' by the existence of the norm itself. Punishment (or reward) is itself contingent upon that norm being enforced—and *that* in turn, as we know from innumerable instances in life and fiction, is anything but a sure thing.

There is a further, disquieting consideration. Even assuming a very high probability that sanctions would be actually applied, that way of reducing the contingency of social reality—society exists in so far as norms operate, but norms *do* operate because the sanction follows upon compliance/violation as nearly as night follows day—is not very reassuring for Durkheim, for two closely connected reasons. In the first place, compliant conduct motivated only by the (near-)certainty that non-compliance would bring swift and painful punishment upon the miscreant strikes Durkheim as morally deficient; a society where such a motivation, and only such a motivation, inspires the great majority of people to compliance looks to him hollow and brittle. In the second place, that motivation is intrinsically a utilitarian one; it entails that most compliant conduct is inspired chiefly, strategically, by individuals' calculation of their own private advantage. This line of thinking places too many eggs into the favourite basket of the economists, the individual's conscious effort to maximize his/her happiness or utility.

On this account, while insisting on the critical significance of sanctions, Durkheim tends to emphasize their symbolic function, and particularly the symbolic function of punishment, as against their role in actually motivating conduct. Whatever it does to the miscreant, his/her punishment also signals to the good citizen that society stands by its norms, reassures her/him as to his/her good moral standing. Also, in the preface to the second edition of *Règles*, Durkheim denies that the sanction is the essential quality of collective representations; rather, it is a visible indicator which makes them recognizable as such: it indicates that society stands behind a norm, expects it to be binding. But compliance with norms, according to Durkheim, must typically rest on considerations other than the calculation of advantage.

The Centrality of 'Ought'

What considerations, then? Durkheim discounts the significance also of those grounded on the individuals' awareness of the necessity that there be norms, of the collective utility of institutions, of the contribution which their own compliance makes to the maintenance of norms and thus to the general wellbeing. Durkheim is, of course, very well aware of these things himself, but he is so *qua* social scientist; individuals at large, in their capacity as actors, would find it very difficult to detect the connection between given norms and societal welfare, and to acknowledge that their own compliance with those norms is necessary to sustain that connection. Such reasonings cannot be trusted to sustain norms (and thus society) in the majority of cases for the majority of people, who mostly experience norms as irksome and sometimes baffling limitations upon their wills, and are likely to be tempted to evade them in the pursuit of their immediate interests. (This line of analysis has been much advanced in current theorizing on the so-called 'free rider' problem.)

What other considerations, then, can induce people to avoid or to resist such temptation? Durkheim's answer is in keeping with one given by a long tradition of Western social thought to the question of the nature and grounds of political obligation. The conceptual centre of the argument can be held by a variety of expressions, such as 'moral bindingness', 'dutifulness', or 'legitimacy'; Durkheim generally signals the distinctive core of his own version of that answer by using the expression 'moral' and its derivatives. My own preference, in formulating that version, is for the expression 'ought' (*sollen* in German, *dover essere* in Italian).

To return to our theme—what *is* society for Durkheim?—I would articulate his own answer as follows. Society is the sum total of norms; it exists in so far as individuals' compliance with those norms is chiefly motivated by their sense that they *ought* to comply with them. If society is to survive, individuals' willingness to do what they *ought* to do must be the critical subjective component of their conduct. As much as possible, that willingness should be supported also by their awareness of sanctions, by ease of habit, by a penchant for orderliness in their lives; but it must be strong enough, if necessary, to override or to dispense with other considerations, such as individual convenience and advantage.

Put otherwise, for Durkheim the answer to what I call his *pathos*—the concern, unease, anxiety, generated by his own understanding of society as a contingent reality, and most particularly by his view of some modern social developments—lies in his sense that people can develop and sustain a capacity for self-transcendence. That capacity is not innate to them: it must be *socialized* into them by educational institutions.

Durkheim took a great interest in education, and his first academic position was in 'pedagogy', an academic subject of philosophical lineage to the cultivation of which he imparted chiefly an empirical orientation. This, so far as I know, took form not as a systematic observation of the educational process 'on the ground' but as a sustained analysis of educational institutions, and particularly of their historical development.[3] The correlation between those institutions on the one hand and on the other the intellectual, political, and social development of early modern and modern France was Durkheim's primary research topic in this field; but the pursuit of it was accompanied by a sustained reflection on 'school and society', and particularly on the contribution that schooling made, or could make, to the construction and maintenance of a morality appropriate to contemporary circumstances.[4]

However, the cultivation of a capacity for self-transcendence should be the concern also of other than educational institutions; and Durkheim regretted that contemporary society seemed reluctant to establish and empower the arrangements needed to do this work for it within the increasingly significant sphere of occupational life. Note, however, that all institutions are themselves 'made of norms', and on that account can themselves only operate by mobilizing a capacity for self-transcendence. For this reason Durkheim holds that the institutions he chiefly recommends for 'moralizing' contemporary social life—officially constituted occupational bodies, as we shall see—should, to begin with, constitute moral environments in themselves.

If self-transcendence is, as I am arguing, Durkheim's answer to his own *pathos*, one may wonder how reassuring an answer it is. Is not self-transcendence rather a mystifying concept, and in any case— whatever it may mean—a tall order?

Let me address both these objections together. Perhaps self-transcendence is a fancy name for something fairly ordinary. Take the concept of role, one which sociologists use most frequently (though Durkheim himself did not). At least in some understandings of that concept, it entails that individuals, *qua* role holders, largely disregard their own preferences as to how to conduct themselves within certain situations, or indeed do not even allow themselves to form or consult such preferences. Rather, they routinely arrange their own conduct to match some dictates which do not originate from themselves, but pre-exist them or at any rate constrain them, being so to speak inscribed within standard scripts, which the role holder takes for granted, and to which he/she hands over control.

If this does not quite evoke the lofty imagery built into the notion of self-transcendence, it may be noted that more sophisticated analyses have revealed a component of some significant roles, the very name for which—role *commitment*—does get quite a bit closer to that notion. For 'commitment' entails a role holder's willingness to forbear from negotiating his/her role conduct with the role partner, to orient it instead to a sense that the holder's and the partner's continuing cooperation is a worthwhile thing in itself, that some sacrifices are worth making to keep the role relationship in being, that the partner deserves to be trusted even though trusting him/her makes the role holder vulnerable—and so on.

Thus the example of the role concept validates—at the cost perhaps of rendering it somewhat banal—the notion of self-transcendence, which I have imputed to Durkheim as a response to the *pathos* aroused by the contingent nature of society. But the example lies at a level of social experience (that of immediate inter-individual interaction, even if nested within larger organizational contexts) to which he pays very little attention, for he prefers to frame his most distinctive and forceful arguments in terms of the conceptual couple individual/society. Even if his view of the particular problems of modern society induces him to evoke an intermediate level between those two, there is basically one such level in his discourse, and it is occupied chiefly by the large, nationwide social entities the establishment of which he deems necessary—the occupational corporations. Furthermore, as we shall see, these are conceived as organic components of the larger society, to be endowed with public faculties and facilities by the state, in its capacity as the central organ of that society and on its behalf.

Twofold Man

The hold on Durkheim's mind of the conceptual couple individual/society is demonstrated also by his repeated argument, already mentioned in Chapter 2, to the effect that 'man is twofold'. The argument is that there are two, and basically only two, sets of representations at work within the individual's mind: those of the individual's own making, which are anchored in his/her own bodily uniqueness, reflect his/her distinctive experiences, and express and serve his/her peculiar interests; and those of society's making. The latter are, so to speak, inflected and differentiated by the individual's group memberships, but once more only the occupational memberships are thematized by Durkheim, and they are not seen as grounding the individual's individuality as much as constituting a distinctive aspect of his/her societal identity.

This vision of 'twofold man' lends itself to two critical comments. In the first place, I find it much less imaginative and convincing than the understanding of the genesis of individuality put forward by another classical social theorist, Georg Simmel, in his essay translated into English as 'The Web of Group Affiliations'.[5] According to both Durkheim and Simmel, the advance of differentiation, accelerated and intensified by modernity, loosens the hold upon the individual of the local group, and allows him/her to become enmeshed in new groupings. But, unlike Durkheim, Simmel notices how diverse these groupings are and how much, with the advance of modernity, memberships in them come to depend on the individual's choice, both expressing and fostering his/her own sense of individuality. Eventually, in the typical modern situation, each individual comes to belong to many changing and intersecting groups each of which shapes and orients him/her in a certain way. However, because those groups are multiple, and variously crisscross one another, it becomes very unlikely that any two individuals, within the same society, will share exactly the same set of group affiliations; and *this*—the idiosyncratic nature of each individual's set—is what grounds his/her individuality.

As I have already suggested, Durkheim seems not to have perceived that the advance of societal differentiation would produce (indeed, had produced, and continued to produce) an increasing number of overlapping, changing settings and memberships. He systematically emphasizes the partitioning of national populations into occupational groupings, directly related to the division of labour, and he occasionally acknowledges the class structuring of populations. He looks forward to a situation where individuals will locate themselves within these groupings, in each new generation, according to their talents. But he treats these affiliations very much as permanent ones for each individual; he assigns to educational institutions the task of preparing individuals for stable occupational memberships, and looks forward to corporations being officially mandated and empowered to assist and discipline the various occupational pursuits. The other partitionings of populations he systematically considers were related to the occupational ones (educational attainment, for instance) or were ascriptive or semi-ascriptive: gender, age, religion, locality. He demonstrates little interest in the phenomenon of multiple, elective, changing, intersecting affiliations of an associational nature, based purely on individuals' values and preferences, and presumably expressing and cultivating their distinctive interests and tastes—and thus, as Simmel would have it, differentiating them from one another. He also has little sense of (and, one suspects, little sympathy for) the pluralization of cultural perspectives, of values, of conceptions of reality, associated with the above changes in the social structure, with the heterogeneity modernity engenders between designs for living, collective and individual, coexisting, but occasionally conflicting, within the same national community and sometimes cutting across national boundaries.

The main exception to this lack of sensitivity was of course Durkheim's sophisticated awareness of the conflicts raging within the France of his time; but one has the impression he considered them chiefly an unfortunate legacy of the nation's past, which he trusted could be surmounted in the near future. Characteristically, he took sides publicly in those conflicts only once, during the Dreyfus affair; the rest of the time he tried to affect them and moderate them from above, so to speak, in the name of science and availing himself of his standing as an adviser to national bureaucratic bodies.

In the second place, whether or not Durkheim can conceptualize modern individualism as satisfactorily as Simmel does, it is not in doubt that he is keenly aware of it, and increasingly concerned about it, as we have seen in Chapters 2 and 4. But modern individualism poses a problem, again, for his thesis about 'twofold man'. This, as we have seen, locates in the individual mind something we could call a primordial individualist component, grounded on the impatient and unreflected needs of 'the primitive constitution of man', which every child at his/her birth reproduces and re-imports into existent social reality. On this component, education in its various forms superimposes a 'social being'—the other half of 'twofold man' (*Éducation et société*, 51). But the advance of the division of labour and, most acutely, of its modern forms introduces a new, derivative form of individualism, strictly (and paradoxically) of social origin, which Durkheim views as chiefly responsible for the much-increased incidence of egoistic suicide. Thus under modern conditions the socialized individual, made aware of norms through education, respectful of the limitations they impose on its activities, and responsive to collective interests which it perceives as higher than its private ones, lies besieged between a primitive and an advanced layer of thoroughgoing, unrestrained individualism. The schematism of 'twofold man' has thus become untenable.

But let us return to our main theme: what is society for Durkheim? We may make more explicit a point resulting from what we last said with reference to that question. If society is constituted not by all minded patterns of inter-individual activity, but only by those evoking in individuals a sense of how they *ought to* act (NB whether or not those individuals conduct themselves accordingly), then minded patterns oriented instead to the pursuit of individual advantage, or resulting from the individuals' awareness of technical rules, are *not* constitutive of society. Society exists in so far as inter-individual conduct is controlled by *ought* considerations, not by considerations concerning what works, or what is advantageous to the individual.

This is a drastic limitation of the concept of society, but it results straightforwardly, I suggest, from two chief arguments made by Durkheim. The first, which he repeated almost obsessively in all manner of formulations, is that society is a *moral* reality through and through. The second, contained in some express pronouncements about the nature of modern society in particular which we have already considered, characterizes society as having at its very centre activities controlled only by considerations of advantage and of technical convenience, and on that very account judges (and deprecates) modern society as being thoroughly and threateningly asocial and amoral. Put otherwise, the typical behaviour of *homo oeconomicus*, considered by the utilitarian tradition the fount itself of society, the mainspring of all progress, and the model for all social conduct, appears to Durkheim to constitute a problem rather than a solution.

Society, then, is for Durkheim the sum total of those collective representations that guide and control the interactions between individuals by evoking in them a sense of moral obligation. It exists in so far as those representations either induce individuals to conform to them or are reasserted in the face of nonconformity by the application of sanctions. It is therefore, inescapably, a contingent reality, which depends on the individuals' willingness to override considerations of personal advantage, to acknowledge the superiority of collective over private interests, or alternatively depends on the effectiveness of arrangements put in place to enforce that superiority. A moral reality itself, society can only survive in and through a multitude of moral acts, including the punishment of moral transgressions, engaged in by the only moral entities that exist besides society itself—individual human beings.

I have repeatedly suggested that this vision of society induces in Durkheim himself a *pathos*, a disturbing sense of the fragility of society itself, which the contemplation of some modern developments renders more acute. That sense, however, is countered in his writings—though never entirely suppressed—by the recurrent consideration of a number of themes. Possibly the most significant one, though not the one he revisits most frequently, is the trust in science. Durkheim sees himself as a protagonist in an intellectual venture of great moment—the development of a novel science: sociology, the science of institutions. The task of this discipline is to identify objectively, through rigorous and compelling inquiries, the nature itself of society, as well as the specific features and requirements of its main types.

In the process, sociology *qua* science acknowledges its own limits. It discovers that the conduct individuals at large must practise in order to produce and reproduce society cannot, itself, be motivated by an explicit, scientifically grounded awareness of its needs, but must flow from a sense of moral commitment to its existence and to its superiority. The upshot of this discovery is the systematic attention paid by Durkheim to four other themes, each focused on one of the main institutions which typically operate to engender, express, and maintain that commitment: education (including the family), political authority, law, and religion. We have already seen that, for Durkheim, a sustained consideration of the processes going on in a further sphere, that of economic life, cannot play the same reassuring role; as I have already suggested, at any rate under modern conditions, the economy is part of the problem, not of the solution. That is, unless and until an express programme of institutionalization and moralization is carried out within that sphere, through reforms whose blueprint Durkheim himself repeatedly sketched out.

Within Durkheim's work as a whole, the problem brought to the fore in this chapter is quantitatively marginal. As I said at the beginning, he explicitly forbears to define society; and the understanding of it I have attributed to him, and the attendant *pathos*, have been to some extent inferred by me, or indeed conjectured. Most of his work attends to the themes mentioned above: that is, it seeks to establish sound scientific knowledge concerning a variety of social phenomena, and particularly about those critical institutions. In the process, he produces or elaborates insights that bear no direct trace of that peculiar understanding of society and of the related *pathos*. Even his work dealing expressly with modern society does not frequently voice the disquiet aroused by the position held within it by economic phenomena, and prefers to emphasize, and to applaud, the growing role played by public authority, and the increasing number and significance of the rights held by individuals in advanced societies.

Yet I would contend that even if mostly Durkheim manfully 'gets on with it', instead of thematizing expressly the contingent nature of society, or the jeopardy of modern society in particular, these distinctive positions of his remain qualitatively central to his whole enterprise; and that only his confidence in individuals' ability to transcend themselves, if properly guided and encouraged by appropriate institutional arrangements, sustains him in that very 'getting on with it'. My argument in this chapter has foregrounded a set of analytical and moral concerns which Durkheim's work mostly keeps where they belong—in the background.

The reader may have noted that this chapter has interrupted a sequence of chapters each referring almost exclusively to a single, major work of Durkheim's: respectively *Règles* (Chapter 2), *Division* (Chapter 3), and *Suicide* (Chapter 4). It is followed by a shorter sequence of two chapters, not devoted chiefly to the examination of a single work, but bringing to bear a number of writings, including those already examined, on the discussion of two sets of institutions in which Durkheim took a considerable interest—legal and political ones.

6

Law

Main Sources

This chapter presents Durkheim's contribution to the sociology of law rather selectively, for it discusses almost exclusively two texts: *Division*, already considered at length in Chapter 3, and a book whose English version is entitled *Professional Ethics and Civic Morals*. The French version (first published as late as 1950, in Turkey of all places) bears instead the title *Leçons de sociologie*.[1] This indicates quite precisely the nature of the work in question—the text of a course of lectures which Durkheim taught several times both in Bordeaux and at the Sorbonne, and to which he himself gave the somewhat archaic title *Physique des mœurs et du droit*.

This limitation of the argument to be conducted below conceals both the quantity and the quality of Durkheim's scholarly engagement with the law as a subject for sociological discourse. That engagement was, to begin with, quite extensive. In particular, Durkheim's great journal, *L'Année Sociologique*, paid a great deal of attention to contemporary works of juridical scholarship, especially French and German ones, and particularly those dealing with the history and with the anthropology of law; and a number of those works were discussed by Durkheim himself, either in his 'Notes critiques' or in original essays.[2] His engagement with law was, furthermore, fairly deep and sophisticated: his writings on the subject exhibit a considerable familiarity with the juridical mode of reasoning and with a number of legal fields. This in spite of the fact that, unlike his great opponent Gabriel Tarde, who was a judge by profession, or for that matter unlike Max Weber, who had qualified for the German bar before becoming an academic social scientist, Durkheim had no formal juridical training. In fact, none of the biographical sources known to me indicates how as a layman he came to be so well informed concerning a field of scholarship which in the France of his time enjoyed high intellectual prestige and held a central position in the French university.

One may also note that law was one of the academic subjects outside the conventional social sciences, in which significant French scholars inspired by Durkheim went on to gain prominent positions while expressly acknowledging his influence upon their own work. (I am thinking particularly of one of the most important public law scholars of the first part of the twentieth century, Léon Duguit.)

Of the two texts on which this chapter draws, *Division* has been much more consistently recognized (and often, one might say, celebrated) as containing a most significant sociological discussion of law. On the face of it, it considers legal phenomena *only* as a convenient resource for identifying another social phenomenon, of more general sociological significance but more difficult to study directly—the solidarity obtaining within a given society. But this, let us say, instrumental approach to law, or its use as an *indicator* or a *proxy* for underlying social realities, while it has its limitations— remarked on by the editors of a useful collection of Durkheim's writings about the law[3]—is in fact accompanied in the text by what seems to me a remarkably thorough and original discussion of the legal phenomenon in its own terms, which emphasizes the variety of forms and contents taken by it, and develops significant sociological insights into its premises and its consequences. In the pages that follow, I shall try to convey some of these insights, a few of which have already been foreshadowed in my chapter on *Division*.

Durkheim's Understanding of Law

In spite of his awareness of the growing body of scholarship, historical and anthropological, documenting the variety of forms taken by legal phenomena outside the modern West, Durkheim entertained a thoroughly modern and Western view of the social function of law, 'the instrument [*appareil*] through which . . . social action is performed' (D 182; *153*).

When society is led to intervene [in the business of individuals] it does not do so in order to accommodate individual interests; it does not seek what might be the most advantageous position for the contendants and does not propose a compromise to them; rather, it applies to the particular case laid before it the general and traditional rules of law. But the law is in the first place a social matter, and its concern is other than the interest of the parties to a trial. (D 81–2; 70)

This is a rather ethnocentric understanding of the social mission of law, for non-Western cultures often make arrangements for finding and applying the law which seek, instead, a compromise with which all parties can live, rather than turning one of them into a winner and the other into a loser. But the understanding articulated by Durkheim was—and to an extent still is—shared within Western cultures, and taken for granted, in particular, by jurists in Durkheim's own time. Durkheim also shared with those the assumption that all the law obtaining within a given society was necessarily a system, an ensemble, however huge and complex, of intrinsically related matters, no matter how diverse and mutable, held together by abstract and general principles valid across all its variety of manifestations. (This conception has become rather less tenable, even in the West, in the course of the twentieth century.)

As with society itself, according to Durkheim the prime task of sociological discourse on law was to acknowledge the essential unity of the phenomenon at hand; the second task was to reconnoitre its internal variety. The key conceptual strategy for concealing the tension between these two tasks—again in discoursing both about society in general and about law in particular—consists in dividing each reality into two parts opposed to one another, but which by the same token are closely related and jointly make up the whole. In *Division*, as we have seen, Durkheim did this for society by contrasting two basic ecological arrangements, two sharply different ways in which a given population could settle over a territory. As to law—which Durkheim conceptualized (rather conventionally) as the sum total of those moral expectations which a society not only lays upon individuals but equips itself for sanctioning officially in case of violation—the nature of the sanction could serve as the criterion of an equally general and abstract division. 'It is suitable to classify juridical norms on the basis of the sanctions attached to them' (D 33; 28).

Sanctions: Repressive and Restitutive

As it happens, conveniently, the sanctions themselves are essentially of two types. One type of sanction—*repressive*—consists in inflicting pain on the violator of a norm backed by strongly and universally felt social sentiments, in order to reassert the commitment to it of the society as a whole. The other type—*restitutive*—applies instead when the norm violated does not express, and is not backed by, strong and universally felt sentiments, but is intended chiefly to protect the private interests of individuals. Here the sanction merely ensures that the violation itself does not bring the violator any unfair advantage: rather, it undoes whatever advantage he/she might have gained in his/her dealing with another individual, and compensates the latter for whatever losses he/she may have undergone as a consequence of the violation.

These two conceptual distinctions can now be brought to bear on one another by means of a further distinction, that between mechanical and organic solidarity. Where the first, segmental type of ecological arrangement prevails, the consciousnesses of the individuals making up the society harbour prevalently similar, precisely expressed, and strongly entertained representations. This, of course, stunts the individuality of the society's components, who are 'mechanically' integrated into the society, and attaches to norms prevalently repressive sanctions. Where, on the contrary, the parts of society do not stand to one another as juxtaposed, homogeneous, largely self-standing segments, but are heterogeneous, both because they differ from one another and because they are in turn composed of differentiated elements, what holds the society together is the 'organic' dependence of each part on all the others. The society still protects its norms with its laws, but the sanctions attached to these are chiefly intended to secure the regularity and reliability of the interactions which the society's parts and their individual components conduct with one another: they need no longer be repressive, but become chiefly restitutive.

There is thus an inner coherence between the prevailing type of law and the nature on the one hand of the ecological arrangement of a given society and on the other of the solidarity obtaining within it. It is this that authorizes, so to speak, the treatment of a predominantly repressive law system or a predominantly restitutive law system as the indicators, respectively, of the mechanical solidarity of segmental societies and of the organic solidarity of post-segmental ones. An obvious corollary is that as a society moves from the one to the other type, repressive law becomes recessive and restitutive law dominant.

Since law represents the principal forms of social solidarity, it is enough that we classify the different kinds of law and then seek to which different kinds of social solidarity they correspond. Currently, there is very likely one kind of law that symbolizes that special solidarity engendered by the division of labour. Given this, in order to measure the extent of the latter it suffices to compare the number of the juridical rules expressing it with the total amount [*volume*] of law. (*D* 32; *28*)

Durkheim seems to be on somewhat shaky grounds when he claims that the above corollary constitutes an empirically established generalization (*D* 108–10; *92–4*). According to a remarkable essay by Sheleff, in a number of significant cases studied by historians and anthropologists, the development was the other way around; at any rate, *some* relatively primitive societies left it to the initiative of their individual members whether or not to seek redress for violations of social norms, and the redress took restitutive rather than repressive (i.e. punitive) form.[4]

Crime and Punishment

In any case, the treatment of law in *Division* presents aspects of interest other than Durkheim's perhaps contestable assertions about a general shift from prevalently repressive to prevalently restitutive law. One most significant aspect, in my view, is his treatment of criminal law, a topic to which he often returned subsequently in other writings, for instance *Règles*, where, as we have seen, he argues, shockingly, that 'crime is normal'. Some components of that argument had already been advanced in *Division*, and can be briefly reviewed here.

Criminal law, to begin with, is repressive law *par excellence*. It establishes and controls the processes whereby a society reacts to the violation of a norm grounded, as we have seen, on universally and strongly entertained sentiments, by inflicting punishment on the violator.

Punishment consists in a passionate reaction, of greater or lesser intensity, which the society inflicts through the medium of a constituted body upon those of its members who have violated certain norms of conduct. (*D* 64; *52*)

Which norms? As we have already seen, those expressing, and seeking to impose upon conduct, universally and strongly entertained representations, 'strong states of consciousness', which evoke compelling feelings throughout society (D 47; 39). But it is not possible to determine objectively and universally the *content* of such representations, and thus the concrete nature of the acts that are criminal in a given society because they violate them. The statement in *Règles*, according to which what is decisive is exclusively 'the prestige vested in some representations', applies here too. *Division* discounts theories which connect the criminal status of certain acts with specific, objectively identifiable interests, whose intrinsic nature induces society to protect them by punishing those who damage them.

A later text—a set of 'theses' Durkheim presented for discussion to the French Philosophical Society in 1906—makes the point quite explicit:

> I am not being punished or blamed *because* I carried out this or that act. It is not the intrinsic nature of my act which entails the sanction. This does not derive from the act being such or such, but from its not conforming with the norm which proscribes it . . . It is the existence of that norm and the relationship the act has with it that determine the sanction. (S&P 60; *43*; emphasis original)

As the table of contents of *Division* puts it,

> The sole characteristics common to all crimes currently or previously recognised as such are the following: 1, the crime offends sentiments found within all normal individuals within the society under consideration; 2, these sentiments are strong; 3, they are definite. Thus, crime is whatever offends strong and definite states of the collective consciousness. (D 408; English translation unavailable).

This position, which perhaps makes of Durkheim a 'social constructivist', is affirmed very strongly in the text. For instance:

> One should not say that an act offends against the common consciousness because it is criminal, but that it is criminal because it offends against the common consciousness. We do not condemn it because it is a crime, but it is a crime because we condemn it . . . [Just as] some things are good because we love them, instead of their being loved because they are good . . . [so] an act is socially evil because a society rejects it. (D 48; *40*)

Furthermore, Durkheim criticizes a view increasingly common in his own times, especially among progressive thinkers, who sought to purge modern criminal law of the sheer vindictiveness of the primitive *lex talionis*, 'an eye for an eye'. According to this modern view, punishment should not be conceived as society's revenge, but is intended chiefly to deter individuals from doing damage to social interests, and/or to separate criminals from the rest of society. The criminal process looks *forward* to the future effects of punishment rather than *backwards* to the offence inflicted on the society's common consciousness.

Durkheim, instead, espouses the conservative view according to which the criminal is punished in order to make him/her *expiate* the violation of strongly and universally entertained sentiments—no matter what other effects the punishment may have:

[Even] supposing that punishment may effectively protect us in the future, we consider that it must be, in the first place, an *expiation* of the past. What proves this is the care we take to ensure that it be precisely proportional to the gravity of the crime, which is only explicable if we feel that the perpetrator must suffer because he/she has done evil and to the same extent. In fact, this proportionality is pointless if the punishment is but a means of defence . . . Even if we ascertained that the perpetrator cannot be in any way deterred [from further violation] we would still feel obligated not to punish him/her to an excessive extent. This proves that we have remained faithful to the principle 'an eye for an eye', although we now understand it in a more sophisticated way than we did originally . . . Punishment has remained what it was for our fathers: an act of revenge and thus of expiation. What we avenge, and the criminal expiates, is the outrage done to morals. (D 55–6; 46–7)[5]

Furthermore,

at the bottom of the idea itself of expiation lies the sense of the satisfaction rendered to some power, ideal or real, which is superior to us. When we demand the repression of crime, we are not seeking a personal revenge for ourselves, but for something sacred, which we feel more or less dimly to exist outside of and above us . . . On this account criminal law not only was essentially religious at its origins, but furthermore retains to this day certain religious features. (D 68; 56)

As to other effects of the criminal process, as we have seen from Chapter 2 Durkheim advances the bold thesis that the most significant effects concern not so much the criminal himself, but the rest of society:

If, when crime occurs, the consciousnesses it offends did not unite to attest to one another that they continue to be at one, that this particular occurrence is but an anomaly, in the long run they could but be shaken. (D 71; 58)

Thus crime brings near to one another the honest consciousnesses and concentrates them. (D 70; 58)

The institution of the power to punish [vested in a specialized apparatus] serves to maintain the common consciousness. (D 73; 60)

In the 1960s, Kai Erikson's *Wayward Puritans*[6] revised and extended this view of Durkheim's by suggesting that by prosecuting and punishing certain activities (including some like witchcraft practices, whose very occurrence is doubtful, not to mention their impact on concrete social interests), a society reaffirms the boundaries of acceptable conduct and evokes the people's awareness of and commitment to them.[7]

The Evolution of Criminal Law

Whether valid or not, these general views about the nature of crime and punishment are complemented in a subsequent text of Durkheim's by a major essay concerning the 'laws of the evolution' of criminal law.[8] Here he proposes two generalizations concerning respectively the 'quantitative' and the 'qualitative' variations undergone by punishment 'in the course of history'.

The first generalization concerns 'the dimension or quantity of punishments': 'The intensity of punishment is all the greater the more societies belong to the less advanced type—and the more their central power is absolute in nature.' The first characteristic refers, essentially, to what I have called the ecological arrangements of society; in other words, punishment is more severe and cruel in societies approaching the segmental mode of organization and less so in societies which distance themselves from that mode. As to the second, 'we call governmental power absolute when the other social functions do not confront it with anything which could effectively moderate and limit it'. Note: 'these two factors of penal evolution—the nature of the social type and that of the organ of government—must be kept carefully distinct, for they do not depend on one another, and act independently of one another, sometimes even with opposite effects.' Thus, even a relatively advanced (that is, differentiated and organically solidary) society may have a fiercely and cruelly oppressive system of criminal law if the government at its centre is not counterbalanced by what we might call today a developed civil society.

The second generalization concerns the modalities of punishment: 'Punishments consisting exclusively in the deprivation of freedom, for a time that varies according to the gravity of the crimes, tend to become more and more the normal type of repression.' Earlier, the purpose of imprisoning criminals was simply to keep them available, as it were, for different forms of punishment; subsequently, imprisonment comes to be conceived as intrinsically punitive and, indeed, as the form of punishment most suitable for a greater and greater number of crimes.

Taken together, these two generalizations might suggest that, as society becomes more and more advanced, it can increasingly dispense with criminal law and with punishment at all. But Durkheim does not believe this to be possible: a process of decriminalization is underway, but it can only go so far.

There is not a general weakening of the whole repressive system; only one particular system weakens, but it is replaced by another which, while being less violent and harsh, still has severities of its own and is in no way destined to a continuous decadence.[9]

Before leaving this topic, I will remark on what I consider a major flaw of Durkheim's analysis of criminal law. It transposes what is perhaps a tenable view of the process of punishment in 'primitive' societies—where punishment can be plausibly seen as a matter of the whole society visiting its displeasure on the violator of strongly entertained normative representations—into a conception applicable to all societies, even large and complex ones, including modern society. He thus fails to take on board the insight articulated by Thrasimacus in a dialogue by Plato:[10] in a divided society laws in general, and thus also laws about crime, always express and sanction the preferences and interests of the powerful, compelling the weak to abide by them.[11] Only in his first generalization about 'penal evolution', as we have seen, does Durkheim consider the role of central power in the criminal process; and even then he brings it to bear exclusively on how often and how harshly punishment is applied, not on *which* acts are declared criminal, prosecuted, and punished, and thus not on *which* interests are privileged and *which* sacrificed.

Furthermore if, as Durkheim rightly holds, the criminal process involves a specialized apparatus, a differentiated part of society, he should have reflected that such apparatus might become interested in increasing its own faculties and facilities, in widening its own discretion and thus potentially its own arbitrium—another possibility that, instead, he never seriously contemplates. Both these serious limitations of his views on criminal law reflect a broader theoretical flaw: Durkheim envisages only a dialectic between the individual, and society as a whole, and does not systematically explore collective subjects located between the two, the respective interests, and the resulting conflicts.

The Institution of Contract

But let us return to *Division*, to emphasize a very significant contribution it makes also to the sociology of private law, that is, that body of norms that attends to and disciplines the legal capacities and activities of individuals and their relations. That contribution, already mentioned in a previous chapter, concerns the prime legal institution of modernity, contract.

The expression itself, 'institution of contract', conveys the main point Durkheim seeks to make in his critique of Spencer's understanding of the contractual phenomenon. If we conceive of contract itself as a relationship established and regulated by the private agreements of parties, rather than as authoritatively imposed or bestowed upon them, we must acknowledge that it is not a self-sufficient reality. Private parties can enter contracts, and can expect them to be reliably executed, and to realize the interests envisaged upon entering, only in so far as they avail themselves of juridical arrangements predisposed and maintained by an apparatus of rules to which they do *not* relate as contractual partners, but as subjects or citizens.

It is the law itself, as—once more—a body of authoritatively sanctioned norms, that establishes who can enter and terminate contracts, what aspects of individuals' total legal position can be settled and modified through contracts, what formalities must be observed if a contract is to be valid, what remedies are available to a party to a contract who sees the other party neglect his/her obligations, and so forth.

The law of contract ... is not just a useful complement to agreed upon arrangements, but their fundamental norm. It imposes itself with the authority of traditional experience, and constitutes the very basis of our contractual relations. We can only occasionally and partially depart from it. (*D* 192; *161*)

In sum, contract is not self-sufficient, but is only possible thanks to a regulation of contract which originates from society. It presupposes it, for its function is much less that of creating new rules than that of instantiating pre-established general rules; furthermore, it can only become binding under certain conditions which it is necessary to define . . . The role of society cannot be reduced to seeing passively that contracts be enforced; it entails also determining under what conditions they become enforceable and, if necessary, to re-establish their normal form. The parties' agreement cannot render just a clause which is not just in itself, and there are rules of justice whose violation must be prevented by social justice, even if the interested parties have consented to it. (D 193–4; 162–3)

Division brings to bear considerations of social justice[12]—at the time, probably, an expression more controversial than it has become since—on two other, related matters pertaining to private law: hereditary succession, which systematically favours some individuals as they take their role within their society's division of labour, and by the same token disfavours others; and the employment relation, which often hides systematic imbalances between one party, the employer, and the other, the employee. But these matters will be considered elsewhere, as aspects of Durkheim's views about modern society.

The Evolution of Property

Here, let us briefly consider the other major text mentioned at the beginning of the chapter, *Leçons de sociologie*. This makes a very considerable further contribution, in chapters 12–18, to the sociology of private law, and particularly of two institutions: property and (again) contract. Although the titles of these chapters (or, more properly, lectures) do not make this clear, these contributions chiefly conduct an analysis of the genesis and development of those institutions *within Roman law*, a subject in which Durkheim had a considerable competence (revealed also in some of his writings in *L'Année Sociologique*).

It is on this ground that Durkheim argues a thesis dear to him, the full significance of which he was to explore in his last masterpiece, *Formes élémentaires de la vie religieuse*. These legal institutions (but not only these: rather law in general, and indeed social institutions in general) were originally religious in nature: that is, all the primordial *manières d'agir et de penser* relating to a given concern, even if today they appear thoroughly secular in nature, expressed the way a society conceived sacred reality and dealt with it in ritual. They only slowly differentiated themselves from that original religious matrix, gaining a greater or lesser degree of autonomy with respect to ideas and practices pertaining to the sacred, and to the personnel attending to the sacred.

Let us see how Durkheim argues this with respect to the right of property. First, he defines it as 'the right a subject has of excluding from the use of a particular thing all other individual or collective subjects' (L 172; 142). He then remarks on the affinity between this form of exclusion and another one, of religious nature, which forbids most individuals to approach, to touch, to make their own, things (spaces, artefacts, social occasions, kinds of people) viewed as sacred. The prototype of this prohibition is the Polynesian taboo, that is, 'the setting apart of an object on account of its sacredness, that is its belonging to the divine sphere' (L 172; 143). But,

between the Polynesians' taboo and the *sacer* [sacred] of the Romans there is only a difference of degree. One can see the close relationship between this notion and that of property. Just as around the sacred thing, in the same way a vacuum is established around a thing which has been appropriated ... In both cases, there are objects which it is forbidden to use or even to touch except to those who fulfil certain conditions; and since, in one of the cases, the conditions are religious, it is infinitely likely that they are of the same nature in the other case. Consequently, one is entitled to suppose that the origin of property is to be found in the nature of certain religious beliefs. (L 173; 143-4).

We may have some doubts about two critical clauses in this statement: 'it is infinitely likely', and 'one is entitled to suppose'. But this text complements a somewhat inferential conceptual argument both by developing further analogies between things sacred and things appropriated (L 177-8; 148-50) and by providing some empirical backing for that argument from the history of law. Building to a large extent on the seminal work done in La Cité antique by his former teacher Fustel de Coulanges (whom he had criticized in Division), Durkheim focuses his attention on landed property, and remarks that under Roman law (although to some extent the same applies to ancient Greek law and to Hindu law, also considered by Fustel),

the family plot of old was impregnated throughout with religiosity, and the rights and privileges pertaining to it were religious in nature. Already its inalienability [i.e. the fact that it could not be bought or sold] proves it, for it is the distinctive marker of *res sacrae* and of *res religiosae*. What else is it, if not a setting-apart even more complete and radical than that implied by an exclusive right of use? (L 178; 150)

110

But there are other indications to the same effect in the bodies of law mentioned above: for instance, the ritual practices required by the plot's proprietor (the *paterfamilias*) to establish or confirm its boundaries, or to legitimate the passage through its gate of a new bride, or the building on it of a new dwelling (*L* 179–80; *150–2*). In sum, Durkheim states,

what makes property into property are religious reasons. From what we have seen, it consists in a kind of insulation that withdraws it from common space. Now, this insulation is the product of religious causes . . . The right of property of men is but a substitute for [*succédané de*] the gods' right of property. It is because things are naturally sacred, that is, appropriated by the gods, that they can be appropriated by people. (*L* 180–1, 185; *152, 157*)

This last passage raises the question of why—like other institutions—the right of property should first be conceived as a religious phenomenon. The text I am discussing gives its own answer, the most concise formulation of which is that, generally, 'religions are the primitive manner in which societies become conscious of themselves and of their history' (*L* 188; *160*); but we will consider a more detailed version of the same answer below, in a chapter on *Formes élémentaires*.

As concerns our topic here, the burden of the answer is that the sacredness of a thing—land to begin with—symbolizes its belonging to the society taken as a whole, which (as we shall see) is the prime embodiment and source of the sacred. In turn, the sacredness of land—originally understood as the seat of the society as a whole— maintains itself even when, in the course of social development, land comes to be distributed among the society's members:

The sacred character vested in the soil . . . is the mark which society has placed on things for the very fact that they are strictly connected with its own existence, they are part of itself . . . All we have said starting from this principle can be conveyed as follows: private appropriation presupposes a previous collective appropriation . . . The individuals have taken over from the collectivity, which is the source of all religiosity . . . Private property was born because individuals have turned to their own advantage, their own use, the respect which society inspires . . . The hypothesis that the group [as a whole] was the first proprietor is perfectly in keeping with facts. (*L* 189–90; *162*)

Durkheim attributes the process of individualization of property (*L* 192; *164–5*) in turn to two processes. On the one hand, the group became more and more identified with its chief, who came to be seen as, among other things, the sole proprietor of the things originally belonging to the group; in this manner the idea emerged that a single person could fully own property, and subsequently other persons began to benefit from it. On the other hand, increasing economic significance began to be attached not to land, but to mobile objects which did not have the same intrinsic relationship to what we might today call the group's identity as the land, and which from the beginning were seen as available for private appropriation:

> With time, with the progress of commerce and industry, mobile property became more significant; it then detached itself from landed property, to which it was originally appended; it began to play a social role independent of that performed by landed property . . . Thus, new centres of property emerged outside of landed property, and which as a consequence did not share its features. (L 194; *167*)

Its novel aspects allowed mobile property to be seen as intrinsically more open to private appropriation and disposal, while allowing it to maintain that inviolability which is the essence itself of property as such, and which—as Durkheim would have it—is a remote reminder of the original sacredness of things appropriated in general.

Before leaving this topic, let me note that a few years before Durkheim began to teach the course of lectures on which I have drawn for this discussion of the development of institution of property under Roman law, Max Weber had written an extensive technical monograph on that very subject, which apparently Durkheim did not know.[13] Weber, however, had related the changes in the juridical treatment of property, and landed property in particular, to the prolonged struggles between significant groups within Roman society over that problem, which had at length to be settled only by the decisive victory of one group over the others. Once more, such a materialist perspective, emphasizing societal division and conflict and the role of power relations, was foreign to Durkheim, who consistently interpreted legal developments (among other things) as aspects of the evolution of society as a whole, and privileged the cultural aspects of that evolution, and particularly the role of religion.

Further on the Law of Contract

Leçons de sociologie contains three chapters on the law of contract, complemented by one on the moral aspects of contractual relations. Here, I shall discuss only the former three, which again take a historical approach to their topic, seeking to identify how the institution of contract came to be in Roman law.

The point of arrival is a situation in which the sheer agreement on a given matter between two actors in the presence of one another, however expressed, suffices to modify the respective legal positions, to generate between them binding obligations and to ground reciprocal, legitimate claims, which the community at large acknowledges as valid and if necessary enforces by bringing sanctions to bear. Durkheim clearly states his basic point about this phenomenon, in terms applicable also to other experiences than the Roman one he knew best:

The idea that the agreement of two wills around one same end could generate obligations for each of the parties constituted a remarkable juridical development, presupposing a great deal of previous advance ... The juridical notion of contract, of the contractual bond ... could only emerge laboriously. Only very slowly societies went beyond the initial phase where all law derived from statutes and superimposed a new law upon that. (L 205; 178–9)

Early on, anything resembling contract as characterized above— that is, any expression of an individual's intent to modify the existing legal situation of that individual and of those others he/she deals with—can only have effect in so far as it is clothed in forms which are religious in nature. The words expressing that will (or consenting to it) must be 'pronounced in religious forms and under religious conditions'; often they include an oath, which invokes a divine being; frequently they must be accompanied by gestures of a ritual nature: 'very often sacrifices, magical rituals of all sorts, come to reinforce the obligatory force of the words thus pronounced' (L 208; 182). The sum of money itself which, under Roman law, the parties often offered as an earnest of their intention to commit themselves for the future was deposited at a temple and called *sacramentum* (L 209; 182–3).

Under these conditions the legal validity of the transaction in question rests chiefly on the ritual correctness of the words used and on the surrounding practices, not on the sheer fact that two parties have jointly *willed* a given modification of their relationship or the initiation of a new one. 'The bond rests on the formula', even when the latter has begun to lose its expressly religious connotations; the resulting transactions remain 'solemn and formal' in nature and to that extent recall their earlier religious matrix. Their solemnity and formality are intended to guarantee that the engagement made by the parties will not lightly be withdrawn and disregarded.

What characterizes [the transactions] is that they are valid only if certain determinate formulas have been pronounced. Nobody can deviate from those, or the contract loses any binding force. But this is a distinctive feature of magical and religious formulas . . . Juridical formalism is but a substitute for religious formalism. (L 212; 186–7)

The Emergence of Consensual Contract

However, the increasing reliance on *verbal* forms, from a certain point on, and the decreasing significance of other symbolic activities, indicates that more and more what matters are the indications of the parties' wills, however constrained they may be in expressing them. 'In this manner the mediating link between the understanding between the [parties'] will and the obligation to abide by that understanding becomes less and less significant' (L 216; 190–1).

At a succeeding stage, when economic development makes transactions more frequent, the formulas themselves become more flexible:

When sales and purchases take place incessantly, when there is not an instant when, so to speak, commerce goes to sleep, one can no longer demand that each vendor and buyer take an oath, have recourse to a pre-established formula. (L 216–17; 191)

But this condition of further evolution toward a mature law of contract is only effective, according to Durkheim, if accompanied by a development of moral nature, reflecting (as we have seen repeatedly) the increasing division of labour and the growing autonomization of individuals. This latter phenomenon, in particular, does not mean only that each individual feels more and more authorized and/or constrained to advance his/her own interest; it engenders also a diffuse sense of obligation to respect the interests of others, and in particular an obligation not to fail the expectations one has engendered in them.

[Already] with solemn contracts . . . if I fail to perform, I disrespect two duties at the same time: first, I commit a sacrilege because I violate an oath, I profane a sacred thing . . . second, I interfere with another person's possessions just as I would if I trespassed on a neighbour's property; I damage him or risk damaging him. But, from a moment when the right of individuals comes to attract respect, I am no longer at liberty to do one of them an undeserved wrong . . . I am bound to the gods by my oath; but I am also bound to another person because my oath, by alienating my word, by externalizing it, allows that person to make it his own as if it were a thing. (*L* 218; *192–3*)

At a certain point this second component frees itself of the first, and grounds the contract proper, called 'consensual' under civil law because it comes into being, and begins to produce its effects, purely on the strength of the fact that two individuals have jointly willed a modification of their respective rights toward one another (*L* 218–19; *193–4*).

It becomes established that the sole declaration of the will, when uttered without reservations, without hypothetical conditions, when—in other words—it presents itself as irrevocable, is irrevocable. From this point it can produce, between individuals, the same effects it did previously when surrounded by formalities; it becomes binding ... While the solemn contract could only come into being through the medium of religious or magical practices, the consensual contract is to acquire the same validity, the same objectivity, exclusively thanks to the law itself .... (*L* 219; *194*)

It suffices that the law declares irrevocable any declaration of will which presents itself as such. (*L* 222; *197*)

A parallel phenomenon is the increasingly restitutive nature of the sanction. Whereas the violation of a sacred, and to a lesser extent of a solemn, contract still provoked sanctions expressing a certain degree of public indignation, irrespective of whether they served to restore legitimate private interests which the violation had affected, when consensual contracts are broken the state intervenes exclusively 'to assure to both parties the full and direct realization of the rights which they had acquired' (*L* 224; *199*).

As this passage implies, a significant aspect of the process is that whereas contracts of old were mostly unilateral, that is, consisted in one party duly promising to do something to the benefit of another, who played only a passive role, the new, consensual contract is generally bilateral. That is, it brings about a true transaction, where two parties exchange either promises or performances, and each expressly or implicitly 'targets', so to speak, the other's—as in the typical Roman formulas, *do ut des, do ut facias, facio ut des, facio ut facias*: I give something to you so that you give me something, I give something to you so that you do something for me, I do something for you so that you give me something, I do something for you so that you do something for me.

In due course this assumption of reciprocity comes to be considered an essential element of a proper, valid contract, as is entailed in the juridical Roman concept *causa* (to which the 'consideration' of common law may be conceptually related). Furthermore,

> consensual contracts came to be necessarily contracts of good faith. One uses this expression for contracts whose content and whose legal consequences must be determined exclusively according to the intentions of the parties . . . (L 225; 200–1)

> [As in the solemn contract] words are generally uttered; but they no longer possess efficacy in themselves because they have lost all religious character. They no longer matter except as expressions of the wills they manifest: consequently what determines the contractual obligations is the state of those wills . . . On that account, for there to be a contract, what chiefly matters is that the parties should have intended it . . . The consensual contract constitutes a juridical revolution. The key role played in it by consent and by the declared will transforms the institution. (L 227; 202–3)

The concern with these matters results from the attention which the mature law of contract (in Rome and elsewhere) devotes to the conditions under which the will has been declared, in order to assure that it is a true, deliberate, freely expressed will. It seeks in this way to secure both the interest of the party making the declaration and that of the other party, who 'in good faith' had relied on the declaration itself. (In archaic Roman law 'it was the letter of the [contractual] formula that determined the engagements of the parties, not their intentions' (L 102; 67).)

The final *Leçons* of the course on 'mores and law' take up the question of the extent to which, under modern conditions, a valid consensual contract need to be not just 'of good faith', in the sense indicated above, but also equitable, in the sense of ensuring an approximate equivalence, an effective reciprocity one might say, between the values of the parties' respective commitments. Characteristically, its title refers no longer to the *law* but to the *morals* of contract, as if to indicate that for the time being the equitableness of private transaction is more an aspiration than an express, duly sanctioned juridical concern. We will consider this argument in another context.

Contract as a Point of Arrival, Not of Departure

I will wind up my discussion of 'Durkheim on the law of contract' by pointing up an aspect of it which in my view possesses considerable theoretical significance. There is a contemporary tendency to construct social processes of all kinds, including the development of institutions, as the result of the mostly unplanned interactions of multiple, independent initiatives taken by sovereign, self-regarding individuals acting exclusively on their own behalf. One aspect of this is the derivation of authority structures from contractual relations—of 'hierarchies', as one says, from 'markets'.[14] The idea is that non-contractual arrangements arise only in order to service, facilitate, and complement contractual ones—say, in order to reduce 'transaction costs', that is, the time and energy contractual partners would need to engage if they were expressly to determine, and to agree upon, exactly how they are to share cooperative, mutually advantageous tasks; they save themselves instead the bother of writing extremely detailed contracts, covering all contingencies, by allowing one of the parties, or a third one, to settle a number of questions on his/her own say-so.

Obviously, one may derive some analytical insights from such a theoretical viewpoint. But it should be said flatly that it is preposterous, in the literal sense that it puts first what came later, and that using it with abandon (as some current variants of rational choice theorising do) can produce more nonsense than those insights can compensate for. The argument on the law of contract in *Leçons* I have just reviewed abundantly proves this. Durkheim, in fact, opens it up by expressing his scepticism about some nineteenth-century versions of the theoretical views I have just mentioned:

The notion of contract is currently considered of such simplicity that one can make of it the elementary fact from which all other social facts can be derived. The theory called the social contract rests on this idea. The social bond *par excellence*, that which unites individuals into the same community, it is said, has been or should be negotiated contractually. And if this turns contract into a primitive phenomenon—whether chronologically, as in Rousseau, or logically—this is because the notion of it appears clear in itself . . . But nothing is more deceptive than this apparent clarity. Far from the institution of contract being primitive, it does not make its appearance and above all it does not develop except at a very late date. Far from being simple, it is extremely complex, and it is not easy to see how it emerged. (*L* 202; *175–6*).

As this passage suggests, the argument Durkheim is about to undertake is different from, and complementary to, the previous argument concerning the non-contractual aspects of contract. It is not only that the institution of contract must have been authoritatively put in place if a network of contractual relations is to arise and maintain itself: the institution itself develops relatively late, through the steps examined by Durkheim himself, with chief reference to Roman law, in lectures 15–17 of *Leçons*, of which I have only given an abbreviated rendering above.

Note that half a century after those lectures were originally given, a notable Italian jurist, Gino Gorla, gave a much more technical and detailed rendering of an argument similar to Durkheim's, grounded on a thorough comparative and historical discussion not only of Roman law and the 'civil law' systems but also of the 'common law' system.[15] It seems odd to me that in the face of such evidence one may continue to consider contractual relations as primordial and as intrinsically self-sufficient, and derive from their own logic all other institutions, including those based on communal feelings and on asymmetries of power and authority.

Individual Rights in General

The part dealing with the state in *Leçons* (to be discussed later) contains also a brief discussion of another aspect of law: the rights vested in individuals vis-à-vis the state itself. Durkheim had a high opinion of the historical significance of such rights. Their proclamation in the American and the French revolutions signalled for him a major, irreversible advance toward the affirmation of the dignity of the human person as a central human value. But he construed those rights differently from thinkers who had viewed them as vested in individuals previous to and irrespective of their involvement in society, and grounded them either—as with Kant—in natural law or—as with Spencer—in an understanding of the socio-historical process as resulting exclusively from the individuals' pursuit of their interest (*L* 101; 66).

For Durkheim, on the contrary,

what lies at the basis of individual right is not the notion of the individual as he/she is, but the way in which society treat and conceives, the esteem in which it holds the individual ... What determines that the individual should have fewer or more rights, these rights and not others, is not because he/she is constituted in a given manner, but because society attributes to him/her a certain value. (*L* 102; 67)

But this, so to speak, moral investment of society in the individual is mediated by the state, which can give it legal expression by sanctioning certain expectations concerning what individuals are entitled to. By establishing a direct link to individuals viewed as the holders of certain claims and obligations, the state progressively frees them from the hold of local memberships, and establishes their autonomy. The individuals' protected expectations grow with the expansion of state activity.

Individual rights are thus evolving; they advance unceasingly, and it is impossible to assign to them a boundary which they cannot surpass. What yesterday appeared as a kind of luxury, will become tomorrow strictly a matter of right. Thus, the task with which the state is charged is unlimited. (*L* 103; *68*)

An implication of this argument is that Durkheim entertains strong reservations concerning the idea of *human* rights, vested in individuals irrespective of their citizenship. As we have seen, it is only through the state that society confers rights on individuals; and each state is necessarily a single, particular polity. Only the merging of all states into an overriding political order, transcending and curbing the claim of each of them to sovereignty, could confer on *all* individuals claims belonging to them as *humans*:

There would indeed exist a theoretical solution to this problem—imagining humankind itself organized as a society. But ... this idea, even if it is not utterly incapable of realization, must be entrusted to a future so indeterminate that it does not warrant taking into account. It is pointless to construe as an intermediate target societies larger than those which currently exist, for instance a confederation of European states. This larger confederation would in turn be a particular state, with its own personality, its own interests, its own physiognomy. It will not be humankind. (*L* 108; *74*)

For the time being, the ground of their protected entitlements is the individuals' citizenship in this or that state; and the counterpart to those entitlements is an obligation Durkheim calls 'patriotism'—'the complex of ideas and sentiments which bind the individual to a given state' (*L* 108; *73*). There is an ongoing cultural process that in all advanced societies promotes a greater and greater awareness of qualities that pertain to the individual as such, a tendency to make of the human person the object of general moral reverence and also of legal protection. But the manner itself in which the human person is conceived is to an extent unavoidably particular, bounded by understandings and preferences specific to a given society.

The theme of these few final comments—the rights vested in

individuals (or perhaps in humans?) vis-à-vis the state—is not often treated by sociologists of law, but is more frequently raised in connection with the topic of the next chapter: Durkheim's contribution to political sociology.

7

Political Institutions

The Place of Political Themes within Durkheim's Work

Forty or fifty years ago, the conventional wisdom concerning Durkheim considered—generally (not always) to some detriment to his 'image'—that his social theory was little concerned with political matters, with the state, government, and policy, and was almost exclusively preoccupied with institutions which belong on the other side of the state/society divide.

This view has since been modified to an extent, chiefly through the revisitation (and translation) of other writings of Durkheim's than those emphasized by earlier interpreters—for instance, his essays on Montesquieu and on Rousseau,[1] or the *Leçons de sociologie*, but also lesser ones, including an article on intellectuals occasioned by the great political *querelle* over the Dreyfus case.[2] Besides this textual basis, the new appreciation of Durkheim's awareness of and interest in political matters has been due to considerable scholarly contributions—notably, two monographs in French on the views Durkheim held respectively concerning politics in general and socialism in particular,[3] and various writings in English.[4]

The contribution of Anthony Giddens, in his collection *Durkheim on Politics and the State*, straddles the divide between textual and interpretative inputs into our theme, for he has edited a remarkable collection of translated writings by Durkheim on political topics, and in its introduction addresses in a particularly purposive manner the question of the dimensions, nature, and significance of Durkheim's interest in politics.[5]

Both Giddens and other contributors to that question, it seems to me, have persuasively corrected the emphasis of previous commentators (and critics) on the conservative aspects of Durkheim's thinking, noting his persistent adherence to republican ideals which in the France of his time did *not* bespeak a conservative orientation, his occasional appeal to ideals of social justice (already noted in my chapter on Durkheim's thinking on law), and the extent to which—as someone has put it—he was 'a socialist of sorts'.[6]

I am less persuaded by Giddens's own emphasis on 'the central role of Durkheim's political thought in his sociology as a whole'.[7] This seems to me a considerable overstatement, explained perhaps, but not justified, by the intent of countering others' inadequate assessment of that role. It fails to distinguish between Durkheim's *intentions*, which may have been to a considerable extent political, and his *attentions*, which in my view were not.

As he reveals in a notable passage (*D* p. xxxix; pp. *xxvi–vii*) Durkheim was motivated in his indefatigable activity as researcher, teacher, and author by an ardent aspiration to make a difference to the current condition of his country, or indeed of European society at large. Of course he was aware that extensive and effective governmental activity would be required for the fulfilment of this aspiration. He had explicit and often articulated views, as we shall see below, concerning the changes to be made in the existing political structures in order to devise and carry out such activity. As an eminent academic pedagogue and as an adviser to the French educational establishment, he was well aware of the role which public authorities had played in the past and would have to play in the future in determining, among other things, the nature and the content of the educational process. Finally, he was deeply attached to the political legacy of the French Revolution, and he was an ardent French patriot.

However, it remains the case that Durkheim did not expressly confront properly political themes in any of his most important works. And this not due just to his sense that 'a sociologist's work is not that of a statesman' (*D* p. xxvii; *1*). Even his corporatist project, discussed below, is expounded chiefly in the preface to the second edition of *Division*, acknowledging that it played no role in the book's original contents, reproduced almost intact from the first edition; in about twenty pages at the end of *Suicide*, where he considers the 'practical consequences' of the previous argument, which is exclusively empirical/theoretical in nature; and in the opening section of his *Leçons*, which were not intended for publication. These widely overlapping texts, in my view, should be considered as a foray into a thematic area which Durkheim did not claim for himself, nor perhaps for sociology at large, although he considered it of great pragmatic significance. Together with others to be mentioned below, those texts amount, in my view, to a significant but not outstanding contribution to modern political sociology.

Durkheim's Political Blind Spots

What blocked Durkheim's path to a more sustained and creative engagement with political reality (including the forms it took in his own time) was chiefly a theoretical flaw to which I occasionally refer elsewhere in this book: an inadequate appreciation of the extent to which historical societies are internally divided, and the groups making them up have unequal resources and contrasting interests, contend with one another, and differ in their ability to realize those interests in the face of opposition.

Of course now and then Durkheim catches sight of these realities; for instance, at the beginning of the lecture where he defines the state, he remarks that any 'political group' presents 'an essential element . . . the opposition of those who govern and those who are governed, of the authority and of those submitted to it' (*L* 79; 42). But note that even here he speaks of the opposition *of*, not *between*, those elements; thus, he emphasizes that they differ from, rather than contrast with, one another.

In any case, when Durkheim mentions phenomena which point to strong contrasts of interest, these seem to be significant for his theoretical enterprise chiefly (if at all) as conditions to be mended. For him, it seems, all cleavages and conflicts between groups can and should be transcended by appealing to, and prioritizing, higher interests which they all share, and which can be objectively identified and effectively pursued if the appropriate institutions are put in place and if they operate as they should.

To put it more directly, Durkheim possessed an inadequate understanding of power and of politics, *if* we understand by the former the asymmetrically distributed ability to assert one group's interest over another's, and by the latter the processes of contention and accommodation whereby from time to time it becomes settled, in a given society, who is going to possess power and how it is going to be exercised. Phenomena related to power and politics in these meanings of the terms—for instance, the making and enforcing of laws, or the formation of public opinion—*are* theorized by Durkheim, but mostly not under those aspects; rather, as dimensions and resultants of the societal 'division of labour', or as distinctive components of modern society in particular.

Some contemporary commentators argue directly against this view, particularly as concerns power. In particular, Lacroix suggests that power relations are a kind of latent but central subject in Durkheim's work, and that this might have become obvious in 'un ouvrage jamais écrit'.[8] I find such a view baffling. I am aware of the fact that one can be deeply interested in power without expressly thematizing the topic and using the concept. Marx, for instance, did not (so far as I know) much discourse about power; but he was eminently interested in power relations, and this is perfectly apparent from his writings. One cannot, in my view, say the same of Durkheim.

The Differentiation of Political Structures

For all that, it remains worthwhile to consider what Durkheim did contribute to our understanding of the political realm. Here, I focus on his understanding of the central political institution of modernity—the state. The background to his more express and diffuse discussion of this theme, in chapters 5–9 of his *Leçons de sociologie*, is constituted by some passages of *Division* which consider the emergence of primary political structures and activities as a significant aspect of the move away from the primitive, segmental ecological arrangement of society and of its replacement by one where differentiated parts engage systematically in mutual exchanges.

There are in fact two aspects to this move which are relevant to our topic. In the first place, even relatively primitive, mechanically solidary societies may witness at a certain point the rise to a position of prominence of some individuals who distinguish themselves by their prowess or their wisdom, establish themselves as chieftains, head huntsmen or judges, and may gain some acknowledged privileges.

This can be seen as the primordial political development, and it is significant because in societies of this kind, as we have seen, there is little or no place for individuality. In fact, Durkheim suggests, the very notion that individuality may be to an extent cultivated, expressed, and recognized was probably validated for the first time exactly in this context. The chief, so to speak, is the primordial individual, the first member of a given society to gain and project a heightened sense of her or his own peculiar endowments and the associated claim to some separateness, some distinction, which allows her or him to exercise, through example or through command, some leverage on the rest of society, some capacity for innovation.

Chiefs are, in effect, the first individual personalities to disengage themselves from the social mass. Their exceptional situation, by setting them apart, endows them with a distinct physiognomy and thus confers individuality on them. Since they dominate the society, they are no longer constrained to follow it in all its movements . . . Thus there has emerged a previously unknown source of initiative. There is now someone who can produce novelty and, to a certain extent, deviate from collective usages. The equilibrium has been broken. (D 172; 143)

In the second place, the formation of relatively depersonalized, institutionalized arrangements not only for leadership but for the routine exercise of authority is a most significant aspect not just of the breach in the primitive equilibrium but of a broader and more significant, ongoing development which progressively transforms the ecological arrangement and all other aspects of the society as a whole. Durkheim characterizes that basic political phenomenon by drawing extensively on the analogy between social development and biological evolution.

The latter engenders new species, each organism of which possesses (indeed, is constituted by) a set of distinctive parts which supply its needs through differentiated activities, each part subservient to the others and to the whole. But this is only possible to the extent that one part of the organism specializes in overseeing and coordinating the activities of all others. In the early phase of evolution this part may be a relatively primitive central nervous system; in the more advanced phases it becomes a brain—a structure that monitors the relation between the organism and the environment, activates the differentiated parts as required, and controls the convergence between their activities.

The State as Society's Brain

It is the brain which, in *Division*, provides the main analogy for the increasingly specialized and developed political structures of a society on the road to sustained, ever-advancing differentiation. These structures stand to the rest of society, and to other parts of it, as the brain stands to the organism as a whole or to its parts. The table of contents goes as far as characterizing 'governmental and administrative functions' as constituting 'the cerebro-spinal functions of the social organism' (411; English translation unavailable). As such, they can only become more and more significant with social advance. Once more, Durkheim attacks Spencer for viewing the units charged with government and administration as remnants of an earlier, 'military' condition of society, which stubbornly and maddeningly resist the fact that social advance, by contractualizing all relations, has made such units dispensable:

On the contrary, [the state's] functions become more numerous and varied the more one attains the superior social types . . . Little by little provisions for the education of youth, for public health, for the administration of welfare activities, for the management of avenues of transport and communication, are brought within the sphere of action of the central organ. It, therefore, develops, and at the same time stretches progressively over the entire surface of the territory a network ever more close and complex of ramifications which replace the pre-existent local organs or make them similar to itself . . . (D 200; 167–8)

The governmental organ grows to the extent that, following the advance of the division of labour, societies come to encompass a greater number of different organs which are more and more solidary with one another. (D 205; 171)

Against this background, a batch of *Leçons de sociologie* develop a much more detailed argument, expressly focused on the state, which raises also the question of its forms and thus ends up proposing an interesting understanding of democracy. Here, Durkheim devoted a lecture to the definition of the state: but this is attained by means of a brief conceptual itinerary concerned at first with what he calls 'the political society'. This is characterized by two aspects: it contains a plurality of diverse groupings (families and occupational groups being the most significant); these all submit to a single authority structure, which does *not*, in turn, derive its powers from any other such structure (L 81–2; 44–6). Within such a society, the state is

126

constituted by 'the special group of the functionaries charged with representing such authority . . . the agents of sovereign authority' (*L* 84; *47–8*).

Already in this lecture Durkheim engages in a more substantial discussion of the state, which, without referring to it, recalls *Division*'s imagery of political authority as the locus of the society's differentiated intellectual and decisional activities, as the society's brain. The state proper (which here Durkheim chooses to distinguish from public agencies charged with merely administrative tasks) is said to be 'qualified for thinking and acting in lieu and on behalf of the society' . Thus 'when the state thinks and decides, one should not say that the society thinks and decides through it, but that it thinks and decides for (the society)' (*L* 85, 86; *48–9*).

In a given political society, parliament and government may well open themselves to inputs from the rest of that society: but they remain the seat of relatively autonomous deliberations, which are likely to differ to some extent from those inputs. Durkheim emphasizes this point. The state

is a group of functionaries *sui generis*, within which are elaborated representations and volition that engage the collectivity, although they are not the work of the collectivity. It is not exact to say that the state embodies the collective consciousness . . . Rather, it is the seat of a special, restricted consciousness, higher and more clear, and more aware of itself . . . The state is a special organ charged with elaborating certain representations valid for the collectivity. These are distinguished from other collective representations by their higher degree of awareness and reflection . . . The state's essential function is to think. (*L* 86–7; *49–50*)

Democracy

This view also frames the conception of democracy proposed by Durkheim in the lectures following those I have discussed so far. Durkheim presents it after disposing of what one might call the 'literal' conception of democracy, which characterizes it as against other 'state forms' as 'the political form of a self-governing society, where government is found dispersed throughout the context of the nation'. Nonsense, objects Durkheim; this amounts to turning democracy into a stateless political society, for 'the state is nothing unless it is an organ distinct from the rest of society. If the state is everywhere, it is nowhere' (*L* 115–16; *82*).

Even the notion that in a democracy the society governs itself through its elected representatives is not acceptable. In the first place, the electoral body excludes women, children, and adolescents, and thus

comprises in reality only a minority within the nation. And since those elected only represent the majority [of the electoral body], in fact they represent a minority of the minority [ils représentent en realité une minorité de minorité] ... (L 111–12; 78)

The number of those who, either directly or indirectly, have wanted [voulu] a given law, never represents more than a very minor part of the nation. (L 139; 107)

In the second place, as we have seen, elected bodies do not function as mere reflections and tools of their constituency, but engage in a process of reflection and deliberation where the views and preferences expressed through the electoral mechanism and other channels of opinion are filtered, pondered, criticized, and often transcended. Durkheim expressly opposes the view of elections as a way of committing the representatives to expressing and conveying specific, non-negotiable demands from their constituents (L 125; 91–2).

Thus far Durkheim associates himself (unknowingly, so far as I can see) with what may be called the 'elitist' critique of the 'literal' conception of democracy: the idea of a self-governing society, of the identity between those who govern and the governed, is not tenable; the business of government is always in the hands of an elite. However, he has little use for a view often associated with that critique, according to which democracy should be seen simply as a mechanism for determining—periodically and in an orderly manner—the composition of the governing elite. Thus understood, he says, democracy would differ from an aristocratic political order only minimally (L 112; 78).

As I suggested above, for Durkheim himself what makes a democracy into a distinctive (and valuable) form of state relates closely to his understanding of the state itself as an organ specialized in thinking on behalf of society. While all states are in the business of thinking and deciding, as we have seen, on behalf of society, democratic ones perform this task by establishing throughout society a variety of positions from which to observe ongoing social activities and in turn to receive social inputs which flow up to the central apparatus. Where this is not done, that is, in non-democratic states, 'the governmental organ is jealously guarded from the sights of the multitude', and

what goes on within it remains ignored. The deep masses of society receive [the state's] action without witnessing, even from afar, the deliberations which are taking place, without perceiving the motives which orient those who govern in deciding their measures. As a consequence . . . the governmental conscience remains tightly localized within those special spheres, which are normally rather restricted. (*L* 114; *81*)

In a democracy, however, the insulation of those spheres is strongly decreased, and communication begins to flow much more freely and regularly between them and the rest of society, in both directions.

Thus the ideas, the sentiments, the resolutions which are processed within the governmental organs are not locked within them . . . Everybody partakes in that *sui generis* consciousness, everybody asks him/herself the questions posed to themselves by those who govern, everybody reflects on them or can do so. Then, through a natural return motion, all the dispersed reflections thus produced react upon that governmental thinking from which they had derived. From the moment when the people poses itself the same questions as the state, the state in order to solve them cannot take no notice of what the people thinks . . . The communications between the state and the other parts of a democracy are frequent, regular, organized. Citizens are kept up to date concerning what the state does, and the state is periodically, or indeed continuously, kept informed about what goes on within the depths of society. (*L* 115, 119; *81, 85*)

This, and not the decision about who is to govern, is the point among other things of *consultations*, that is, of recurrent electoral exercises. What makes them necessary is the fact that the state has ceased to be what it used to be, 'a kind of mysterious being on which the populace did not dare to lay their eyes'; its agents are no longer treated as sacred; 'the state has lost, little by little, the transcendence which made it stand wholly apart' (*L* 115; *81–2*).

Democratic Communication

Essentially, then, what makes a state democratic is the fact that next to it and around it there exists what we would call today a 'public sphere', a complex of structures and processes which allow the population to keep itself informed about state action and to inform the state in turn. Two-way communication is the essence of democracy.

But it is complemented by another trait: the state has ceased to concern itself with a limited and fixed number of matters; the sphere of its action has grown considerably, and is susceptible of ever new extensions. 'Democratic societies . . . are more malleable, more flexible, and they owe this privilege to the fact that the governmental consciousness has grown and has come to encompass ever more objects' (L 117; 84).

However, in keeping with Durkheim's understanding of *all* government as an organ for thinking and reflection, and thus in the first instance as an information- and knowledge-processing organ, the key trait of its democratic form remains the one first mentioned above:

The closer the communication between the governmental consciousness and the rest of society, and the more this consciousness grows and attains new objects, the more the society is democratic in character. The notion of democracy is thus defined by the maximum development of that consciousness, and to that extent determines that communication . . . Thus understood, democracy appears to us as the political form through which society attains a more direct [*plus pure*] consciousness of itself. (L 118, 123; 84, 89)

On this account, Durkheim connects the development of democracy with trends whose advance, for a relatively long time, has modernized European societies: 'Democracy is not something discovered or rediscovered in our century. It is the character which societies increasingly acquire.' The recourse to deliberate and reflected activity on the part of government, and its greater range of objects, is a response to the increasing complexity and changeability of modern society and culture. At the same time, 'in effect, democracy, defined as we have defined it, is the political regime more in keeping with our current conception of the individual'. It represents, to this extent, a moral demand and a moral achievement of modernity (L 123–4; 89–90).

Durkheim does not make it explicit, but this last point suggests a connection between democracy and those ever-expanding rights of individuals which I briefly considered at the end of the chapter on law. Some of those rights (e.g. those pertaining to the freedom of opinion or expression, and of organization) are implied by the institutionalization and expansion of the public sphere. More generally, the modern view of the individual emphasizes autonomy, the capacity for self-determination in response to social demands; and autonomy can only be achieved and maintained when the rationale for those demands is critically tested and accepted. Once more, this requires that the demands themselves, in so far as they originate from public authority, should be, and should be seen to be, the product of deliberate, reflected action, which individuals have a chance to observe and to make an input into.

This is what makes democracy morally superior. Since it is a regime based on reflection, it allows the citizen to accept her/his country's laws in a more intelligent, and thus less passive manner. Since citizens constantly communicate with the state, this no longer represents for them an external force, compelling them in a wholly mechanical manner. (L 125; 91)

Dangers of Democracy

This notion of democracy, which emphasizes the ease with which the citizenry can have access to information concerning state activity, and can in turn make inputs into future activity, suggests a possibility that worries Durkheim. Social demands can become too numerous, volatile, and contradictory, and can thus impede the very process of reflection and deliberation which he sees as central to the institutional identity of the state, and which democracy should render more aware of social circumstances and needs, and thus more sophisticated. They can thus on the one hand commit the state agencies to too many tasks, and on the other render their actions less informed and less effective, and turn the state itself into a body at the same time invasive and torpid.

This worrisome possibility can be avoided if the state is protected from too direct and impatient pressures from the citizenry, and 'the nation'—as Durkheim says at one point (L 125; 92)—can be kept from engrossing the state itself. To express this point in terms Durkheim does not use, but which recall some versions of the theory of mass society,[9] the political elites which, as we have seen, constitute the state for him must be protected, allowed to preserve a measure of distance from the society at large and autonomy with respect to it. This operation does not require disempowering or manipulating the masses; it can be performed by interposing between the state and the masses some arrangements for intermediation, which would function, as it were, as way stations in the two-way communication process we have discussed above.

The ideal arrangement would consist in publicly establishing groupings with which the great majority of individuals identify, and which would on the one hand sense and interpret their needs, thus transmitting to the state credible and responsible demands to which to respond with its policies, and on the other take responsibility for ensuring the same individuals' compliance with directives issuing from the state, even when such directions lay obligations upon them.

The Political Role of Occupational Groups

I have thus introduced, by making use of statements Durkheim made in the central part of *Leçons*, a very significant argument which he develops at considerable length in three texts mentioned at the beginning of this chapter: the opening part of the *Leçons* themselves, the preface to the second edition of *Division*, and the last chapter of *Suicide*. As I have already noted, there is much overlap between these texts, but if one had to choose the most authoritative, the second would probably qualify, since it followed the version in *Suicide*, while the *Leçons* version was never edited by Durkheim, but published posthumously with the rest of his course on *Physique des mœurs et du droit*.

In substantive terms, one might consider the version from the preface to *Division* (second edition) as an extension of the anti-Spencer argument which that book developed in both its editions. There, as we have seen, Durkheim had criticized Spencer on various grounds, including his inability to understand how necessary it was that, in spite of the growing significance of contractual relations in modern society, the state should not only remain in business but increase the range and volume of its operations, in order to secure societal interests that contracts could not encompass—including the creation and enforcement of the law of contract itself. Also, the discussion of anomalous forms of the division of labour in book iii of *Division* had considerable implications for state action, intended (as I mentioned in my chapter on law) to realize principles of social justice.

The preface to the second edition raises by a notch the attack on the political preferences associated with utilitarianism, for it strongly recommends some positive *public* action to monitor and regulate the economy, remedying the damages its present, anarchic condition inflicts on society at large. I emphasize 'public', because this text introduces a remarkable twist: the primary subject of such action need not, and indeed should not be, the state itself, but rather a set of occupational groupings, purposefully instituted and entrusted with faculties and responsibilities of a public nature.[10]

Why so? Essentially, because economic conditions change rapidly, under the impulse of varying market circumstances and of unpredictable technological developments, which the agencies making up the state are ill equipped to ascertain and evaluate. If left to them, the changes in regulation and in public policy which those conditions require would be tardy or otherwise inadequate. Besides, a state vested with too many economic powers runs the risk of becoming tyrannical, for under modern conditions the economic resources and interests of individuals decisively affect their total social position; while acquiring and managing those resources and pursuing those interests individuals should not be exposed to too much pressure from such a distant and overwhelming authority as the state itself.

A nation cannot maintain itself unless, between the state and the private individuals [particuliers] there interposes itself a whole series of secondary groups close enough to individuals to attract them strongly within their own sphere of action . . . Occupational groups [groupes professionnels] are suited for performing this role, and indeed destined for it. One can thus understand how important it is that they, above all within the economic sphere, cease to be as insignificant and disorganized as they have been for a century, in view of the fact that occupations today absorb the greater part of collective forces. (D p. xxxiii; pp. liv–lv)

Instead, economic life should be monitored and regulated on a decentralized basis, by relatively autonomous bodies which organize people according to their location in society's division of labour, that is, according to their occupation. Such bodies would have to be constituted according to the prevailing articulation of the national economy not just into various branches (agriculture, commerce, and industry) but into various sectors of each, as well as the liberal professions; and would comprise representatives of both employers and employees.

It would be their task to ascertain the working conditions obtaining with individual trades and industries, assist in setting salary levels, and avoid the recourse to strikes and lockouts, assess the opportunities and risks presented by current technological and market developments, secure fair competition between firms but also set boundaries to it, if this is necessary to avoid, say, the disruption of a given industry by sudden, wholesale technological innovation.

It would also be the task of such bodies to make sure that all individuals involved in a given branch of economic activity, as employers or as employees, possess both the appropriate skills and resources, and a sense of responsibility toward the trade itself on the one hand and the general public on the other. To this end, they should be empowered by the state to sanction activities which violate those responsibilities.

Such bodies would, then, interpose themselves between on the one hand the state, which would preserve its unique position as the sovereign custodian of the national interest and as the fount of the law, and on the other hand the multitude of individuals, or the organizations formed by individuals exclusively to pursue more effectively their private interests. They would thus help remedy the tendency of modern conditions to atomize individuals and/or to sharpen their egoism, providing society with a visibly configured structure, which bridges the gap between the summit of it (the state) and the base (the population at large).

Those bodies, furthermore, would be both authoritative and well informed. They would on the one hand express and foster the interests specific to the field of economic activity within which they operate and on the other acknowledge interests broader than those— the interests of the consumers, the interest of the broad public in having an economic system where major changes are introduced advisedly and with due regard to their larger consequences. Above all (although Durkheim is somewhat reticent on this point) they would temper and moderate the class struggle, keeping it from damaging a given sector of the economy, the economy as a whole, or the society at large. In sum, they would safeguard and promote the form of solidarity typical of modern society, the organic solidarity based on the awareness not of similarity but of difference, and of the complementarity between differences.

A Corporatist Project

A few comments on this bold institutional design. First, it is significantly (though perhaps not obviously) connected with what I have called earlier the society's ecological arrangement. According to

Durkheim, under modern conditions the location of individuals and groups in a particular part of a society's territory is of decreasing importance; instead, what matters more and more is their position in the occupational system, which largely establishes their identities and determines their interests. People of course remain physically attached to given localities, and this holds also for economic activities; but the territorial reference is more and more a background matter, often of little substantive significance, among other things because of the much-increased geographical mobility of individuals and of economic units.

Durkheim's institutional proposal is perfectly in keeping with this development, and seeks to give it public recognition, enabling society to acknowledge and act upon the new priorities characteristic of the second type of ecological arrangement. Currently, he argues, the political system, being structured chiefly with reference to territorial units (the electoral constituencies coincide with seats of local governments and of peripheral state agencies), fails to give that development the recognition it deserves.

Great public issues generally concern, today, the support to be given to this or that kind of industry or the returns of people's occupational activities; thus the ways of handling them are relatively indifferent to territorial considerations, while these remain critical for the selection of administrative and political elites. This situation would be much improved if the territorial layout of the system were complemented, or should we say cross-cut, by a country-wide structure based instead on occupational differentiation, whose articulations are sensitive to the issues in question, can bring to bear on them a definite competence, and are provided with appropriate public faculties and facilities.

Since the market, from being local as it was, has become national and international, the corporation must acquire the same dimensions. Instead of remaining limited to the practitioners of a given town, it must reach out to comprise all the members of an occupation, dispersed as they are over the territory as a whole ... Since [what they have in common] is independent, for certain purposes, of any territorial determination, it is necessary that an appropriate organ be created, which would express it and regularise its operations. Given its dimensions, such an organ would necessarily be in contact with the central organ of collective life, for events significant enough to involve a whole branch of industrial enterprises within a country have necessarily highly general repercussions which the state cannot but take notice of, and intervene upon ... But these two organs, while related, must remain distinct and autonomous; each has functions which it alone can fulfil. If it falls to governmental bodies to lay down the general principles of industrial legislation, they are not competent to diversify it according to the different kinds of industry. This diversification is the corporation's proper task. (*D* pp. xxvii–viii; p. *li*)

In the second place, Durkheim's proposed design is self-consciously backward-looking, in the sense that it aims to restore, however selectively, some aspects of pre-modern, *ancien régime* society. The recognition of public status for collective entities based on individuals' occupational identities would undo one of the most significant outcomes of the French Revolution, the abolition of all corporate entities by the *loi Chapelier*. The occupational bodies envisaged by Durkheim, like the guilds and corporations of old, would pursue not only strictly economic and occupational goals but also political and moral ones. In particular, it would be their task to promote and sanction 'professional ethics', and this not just in the practice of professions proper but in all manner of economic activities.

Durkheim, however, never conceived of his proposals as entailing a wholesale restoration of pre-revolutionary arrangements. In particular, he was aware that in medieval and early modern times corporate institutions had favoured the maintenance of obsolete and unjustified privileges, hindered the application and science and technology to productive activities, stifled private enterprise, and thus variously impeded progress. In his view, these deplorable aspects of the corporate system of old should and could be avoided while seeking to rediscover and re-enact its positive aspects. In particular, occupational identities could be acknowledged and given public significance, in modern political systems, without renouncing the advantages of a generalized form of citizenship which would assign to all individuals, within a body politic, some rights and duties of considerable significance.

Third, Durkheim's proposal is one of many made in his own times and later in order to give public recognition to the significance of economic problems and of the occupational structure of contemporary societies, and to solve in an orderly and purportedly equitable manner the related distributional problems; a generic name for such attempts is (neo-)corporatism.[11] Their common content can be simply stated.

Economic pursuits are central to modern society, and on them are grounded identities and interests of great significance. They tend to induce conflicts, both over the ways in which different actors can be brought together in productive activities and over the ways in which the product of their cooperation is to be distributed. Market processes alone cannot be trusted to settle those conflicts in an uncontentious manner, because technological change can always destabilize previous settlements, and because frequently the automatic workings of the market have socially damaging effects.

On the other hand, the market should be protected from attempts to destroy it in order to advance the class interests of employees, for such interests are divisive, foment an unacceptable amount of strife and disorder, and undermine the pursuit of broader interests, especially those of the nation as a whole. The state, as the guardian of national interests, should safeguard the market, but at the same time complement and control its operations, and reduce those damaging effects, by empowering expressly constituted public bodies to oversee and to an extent direct national economic life as a whole, as well as to protect the legitimate interests of employers, employees, and consumers.

Many proposals to this effect were put forward, over the last century or so, by various political forces and movements; and the controversies concerning these (particularly when their proposals were officially implemented, whether wholly or partly, whether successfully or otherwise) have mainly ignored proposals of a more exclusively scholarly nature, such as Durkheim's own, which long remained the concern only of historians of social thought.

Durkheim himself, as we have seen, insisted on the distinction between corporations and other public bodies and agencies, beginning with the state. But he did not conceal the fact that his proposal had direct and substantial *political* significance: 'One may even assume that the corporation is called upon to become the basis or one of the essential bases of our political organization' (*D* p. xxxi; p. *liii*). However, apart from commenting on the diminishing significance of the state's territorial articulations (and the related social memberships and concerns), he did not make clear what dislocations would occur in the existent 'political organization' as the corporation established its own presence in it. In particular, so far as I know, he had next to nothing to say on political parties, on the extent to which their competition, within the electoral context and outside of it, expresses social cleavages and conveys contrasting collective interests, and on the potential impact on their role of the re-establishment of corporations.

This silence is one aspect of the lack of sensitivity to and interest in *politics* I have attributed to Durkheim at the beginning of this chapter. It relates to another flaw in his thinking: the failure to take on board the fact that individuals have multiple affiliations (and perhaps identities, to use a fashionable term),[12] that these change in the course of an individual's life, and that under modern conditions the affiliations open to individuals, especially but not exclusively on an associational basis, tend to become more and more numerous, to cross-cut one another, and often to conflict with one another. He resolutely asserts that 'the groups that are durable, those to which the individual devotes his/her whole existence, those to which he/she is more strongly committed, are occupational groups' (L 130; 96–7) —and that is that.

This view may have been more tenable in Durkheim's own time than it seems in ours, for in our own times what one might call the *flimsiness* of many occupational affiliations and of the related employments has become quite apparent. In any case, that view strongly influences the design of his corporatist project, which connects the state chiefly (if not exclusively) with strongly entrenched occupational bodies, conceived as organs of the whole society, which derive their constituencies, their competencies, their responsibilities directly from the division of labour. As we have seen, Durkheim had a strong sense of the significance of a public sphere, and related to it his whole understanding of democracy; yet it is not clear what role that sphere can play once a country's 'political organization' has been redesigned not just to re-establish but decisively to re-empower the occupational groups.

Civil Society

If this is so, then one should not, today, overstate the extent to which Durkheim's thinking can be brought to bear on the fashionable concept of 'civil society', at any rate as concerns its political implications. In his comments on a book by P. Milioukov on the history of Russian Civilization, Durkheim uses the concept of society in the way in which that of civil society is currently used in a political context, that is by coupling it with and counterposing it to that of the state (and sometimes to the market[13]). His opening statement is straightforward:

What is peculiar about the social organization of Russia is that it is entirely the product of the state. Among the Western peoples of Europe, the state has, instead, resulted from the spontaneous development of society; there, political organization has emerged little by little, under the influence of the country's economic, demographic, and moral conditions. The historical process has unfolded from the bottom up. In Russia, the inverse order has been observed: there the state organized itself before society, and (subsequently) it organized society. It was the political structure that determined the social structure.[14]

This statement is, so to speak, politically promising, in so far as it suggests that in Western Europe (civil) society remains, or *should* remain, in a dialectical relationship to the state it had originally brought into being. There are other suggestions to that effect in Durkheim's writings, and some have been mentioned in this chapter. But his corporatist vision, with its tendency to settle authoritatively the question of which social groups matter, and to equip them with unique public faculties, belies that spontaneity of social developments which Durkheim attributes, above, to Western Europe. Also, his inability or unwillingness, once more, to theorize *politics* as an open-ended process wherein groups embodying different interests compete in order to generate, appropriate, and wield *power* and to determine policy deprives that vision of society of substantial political significance. Durkheim is very concerned to establish, so to speak, institutional hinges between the state and society; but his conception of those hinges, or for that matter of the state and of society themselves, is essentially an organic one.

Let us sum up. Expressly political concerns were somewhat marginal to Durkheim's main intellectual enterprise, for reasons both theoretical and moral. However, he did devote considerable attention to political matters, and especially to the central political institution—the state. His conception of both the state and one of its forms, democracy, builds upon the insight already attained in *Division*, according to which political arrangements emerge in a differentiated society chiefly because they are required in order to monitor and supervise the cooperation of its parts. Durkheim's understanding of democracy (we might label it 'cybernetic') is particularly forceful; it is complemented by an expressly political blueprint, whereby officially constituted occupational groups, availing themselves of public facilities and faculties, would assist and complement the process of sustained two-way communication between the state itself and society in which democracy itself consists.

But again, this project is predicated upon a view of the state itself as the intellectual and decisional organ of the whole society; and this view prevents Durkheim from perceiving, or at any rate from theorizing expressly, the possibility that the state deals with society in a predatory manner, instead of servicing its needs, and/or that it can be used as a critical resource by a part of society in order to impose its own interests and preferences upon other parts. He was also little disposed to theorize the process whereby, in a given society, groups compete over the control and employment of the political machinery. His attention, in so far as he deals with political matters, is exclusively attracted by its institutional aspect; and this significant but limited focus, together with other aspects of his political thinking, renders it less useful than it might be in theorizing the relationships between (civil) society, the public sphere, and the state which are characteristic of the modern era and in particular of liberal-democratic political systems.

For all this, I suggest that Durkheim's corporatist project, inadequate as it was as a practical proposition, and theoretically flawed, conveyed and responded to a very substantial problem which his society had in common with ours: how to control or to balance the market without abolishing it or seriously damaging its operations; how to deal with the huge accumulations of economic power which the market allows to form, whether because or in spite of its basic institutional design. Today the problem is posed chiefly by the business corporations (which are of course a very different animal from the corporations Durkheim hoped to bring back into the industrial scene) and to a lesser extent (in my view, to a lesser and lesser extent) by unions; and it is intensified by what we commonly call 'globalization'.

Durkheim had little sense, understandably, of the specific manifestations and dimensions of that problem in our own time. But he posed it squarely, and saw that it required a *political* response. Under this particular aspect, his contribution to political sociology, although in my view limited and perhaps flawed, contains a lesson very much worth remembering.

8

Religion

Two States of Consciousness

Throughout his work, Durkheim presented to his reader numerous pairs of concepts intended to capture the richness and diversity of social life, but also to render more dramatic the contrast between alternative ways of experiencing it, of organizing it institutionally, and of rendering it intellectually. We have already seen some of these conceptual duos: individual and society, compliant and deviant conduct, cohesion and regulation, mechanical and organic solidarity, *homo duplex*, and so on.

A further contrast recurs occasionally in Durkheim's writings in various formulations, until it becomes central in his last masterpiece, *Les Formes élémentaires de la vie religieuse* (1912): the contrast between two *states*—two sharply different ways in which the society can exist and be experienced. The expression 'state', as used here, is analogous to that used in physics, to point up that one and the same substance can present itself in ways as different as a gaseous, a liquid, or a solid state (think of H_2O respectively as vapour, water, or ice). Durkheim himself, in a passage of *Formes*, uses a related expression from that same universe of discourse, *état libre*, 'free state'—a condition in which a given chemical element displays more visibly its distinctive properties (F 302; 214). (Interestingly, Max Weber frequently used a related Latin expression, *in statu nascendi*, in a similar context.) But a more proximate analogy is probably constituted by such an expression as 'state of mind', which Durkheim directly echoes in speaking frequently of *états de conscience,* 'states of consciousness'.

An early formulation of the contrast in question has been mentioned in Chapter 2, drawing on *Les Règles de la méthode sociologique:* collective understandings of reality and perspectives for action can present themselves as mere *courants,* as energetic and compelling but unstable and, so to speak, disembodied flows of opinion and judgement, or as instituted, crystallized, sanctioned *manières d'agir et de penser.* At that stage, Durkheim acknowledged the significance of the former phenomenon, but on the whole preferred to emphasize the latter, for various reasons: in particular, I have suggested, because juridical norms, embodied in texts and backed by enforcement agencies, appeared to him as *the* most prominent and significant social facts.

However, this methodological preference could not be sustained while Durkheim studied suicide and other forms of deviance: norms preserved for him the status of social facts *par excellence,* but he found himself compelled to analyse phenomena which are anti-normative in nature, such as the *courants suicidogènes.* These are, of course, however paradoxically, related to a society's norms structures; but his concern with them caused Durkheim to adopt an imagery which emphasizes moral atmosphere rather than moral structure, diffuse states of feeling rather than publicly sanctioned expectations.

In *Formes,* while he continues to hold that 'institutions are the distinctive fact about human societies' (F 523 n. 1; 370 n. 29), Durkheim appears less interested in exploring the variety of arrangements institutions impose on social life and the related variety of their internal constitution. His focus is, of course, on one major institution only—religion itself—and a central plank of his theory is that religions are all, for their diversity, made of the same cloth. Thus the essential features of all can be determined by analysing closely the most elementary religion we know of, Australian totemism.

This analysis in turn finds much room for the subjective experiences, the distinctive states of feeling associated with religious phenomena; and these are seen to lie not only downstream but also upstream from those phenomena. To anticipate an example to be considered more closely later: although typically ritual practices evoke in the participants, *qua* members of a collectivity, particularly strong states of consciousness, under very special circumstances these can be of such intensity that they themselves *generate* such practices, invest them with their peculiar significance and validity, make them binding for future conduct.

All religion, as we shall see, revolves around 'the sacred'; but the quality of sacredness is itself necessarily attributed to objects, material and mental (conceptions of reality, patterned forms of conduct, places, artefacts, moments in the year, phases in an individual's existence) which do not intrinsically warrant it, but must have it superimposed upon them (*F* 461 ff., 492 f.; 327 ff., 348 f.). Now, this superimposition is necessarily, for Durkheim, wrought by extraordinary, especially strong states of consciousness, on which it falls (or, rather, it fell, in circumstances so remote that they are now veiled from memory and recollected only in myth) to—so to speak—*colour sacred* this or that thing or practice, instituting it as the carrier and instrument of future religious experiences.

We thus have a further Durkheimian duality, within the domain of strong states of consciousness: those which engender institutional arrangements, and those which are engendered by them. This duality echoes perhaps one recurrent in French political theory: *pouvoir constituant* versus *pouvoir constitué*. It presupposes a broader duality, between that domain as a whole and a contrasting and complementary one, presumably comprising weak states of consciousness—which, however, Durkheim does not positively characterize, preferring to treat it as a residual category.

This is possibly because this second domain is very diverse, whereas the former one finds its unity in the peculiar intensity of the subjective experiences it comprises, an intensity which often Durkheim suggests by means of the expressions 'effervescence' and 'effervescent'. For instance, Durkheim says that a ritual feast may generate a controlled, regulated tumultuousness, but *le tumulte réglé reste un tumulte* ('a regulated commotion is still a commotion': *F* 309; 218). It is also unified by the fact that those strong states of consciousness are generally entertained in common, are intrinsically collective; in fact, it is this that makes them strong, the fact that they resonate across individual consciousnesses. On the other hand, weak states (I repeat: so far as I know Durkheim does not use this expression, though he gets close to it in some statements I shall soon quote) are private to the minds harbouring them.

This contrast is suggested by the passage that follows:

those manners of acting to which society is attached strongly enough to impose them to its members ... are elaborated in common ... Thus the representations which express them within each of us possess an intensity unattainable by purely private states of consciousness, for they are strengthened by the innumerable individual representations which have gone into forming them ... In one word, when something is the object of a state of opinion, the representation each individual has of it derives from its origins, from the conditions under which it arose, an energy [*une puissance d'action*] which is felt even by those who do not submit to it. (F 297; 209–10)

According to this passage, the might of collective feelings strong enough to institute a practice, or to generate a particular way of conceiving or judging a given aspect of reality, may reverberate downwards, make itself felt again and again under the different and varying conditions on which that practice or vision is to be subsequently brought to bear.

This is one of many passages in Durkheim's writings which, presumably under the impetus of his moral aspirations, formulate in general terms statements valid at best under restricted circumstances. It is thinkable that a particular ritual ceremony, each time one of the aboriginal clans studied in Durkheim's sources performs it, may evoke in the participants feelings similar in nature and intensity to those which, in time out of memory, inspired those who first conceived it and instituted it. But this is much less likely to be the case when a juridical rule is concerned, or the workings of a particular organizational arrangement for performing this or that mundane task. In such cases, even when individuals comply with what is expected of them out of a sense of moral obligation, their compliance is less likely to be accompanied by a fervent feeling of fellowship, of continuity with past generations; instead, we are likely to be outside what we have called the domain of strong states of consciousness.

However, as I have already indicated, Durkheim has little to tell us about the complementary domain, and that little has a negative, one might almost say a deprecating, tone. This is how he characterizes those stretches (presumably the most recurrent and long-lasting) of aboriginal life when the clan is *not* assembled in order to carry out cultic ceremonies:

Within this ... phase, economic activity is preponderant, and is generally of very low intensity. Gathering grains or herbs necessary as food, hunting or fishing, are not occupations which may arouse particularly lively passions. Society finds itself in a state of dispersion which renders existence uniform, humdrum and dull [*terne*]. (F 308; 217)

Of course, Durkheim did not directly transpose this rather slighting view of economic pursuits from the context of preliterate, tribal existence to that of more advanced societies. As we have seen, he characterized as 'essentially industrial' the European societies of his time, and knew how intense, varied, demanding, and stressful was the social existence associated with their industrial nature. In *Suicide* he indicated that the frequency of self-inflicted deaths varied according to the seasons and the months and the time of day, and was correlated with the intensity of commercial and industrial pursuits. But he saw a deep qualitative difference between the intense social life engendered by those pursuits, which set individual against individual and class against class, and the intense social life associated with clan ceremonies, which periodically unite individuals in the performance of ritual practices.

It was only the latter kind of intensity—choral, not divisive; oriented to tradition, not to innovation; celebrating commonality, not expressing egoism—which he saw as associated, once again, with strong states of consciousness. The former kind of intensity was purely a by-product of the busyness of individual actors. These no longer had an opportunity to experience such states, for on the one hand the relations they entertained with one another were loose and impermanent, and did not presuppose or generate a deep sense of mutual belonging; on the other hand all actors *qua* economic actors operated—each on his/her own account—in a sphere of existence which acknowledged no binding norms, but only considerations of convenience and advantage.

Indeed, as we have seen, under modern conditions economic life, intense as it might be, continued to share a feature Durkheim attributed to it under tribal conditions: it was normatively underregulated. Participants engaged in it on behalf of interests peculiar to themselves, in seeking which they were guided almost exclusively by instrumental considerations which determined, under varying circumstances, whom they could do business with on what terms. The trouble was, as suggested previously, that in the modern world economic activity so practised had displaced other aspects of social life, imposed its own supremacy over them, and was thus threatening to deregulate the social process at large.

Durkheim once confessed to an associate that he felt less and less at home in a society so constituted, while he experienced a sense of familiarity with societies he had never seen, but knew chiefly through the reports of anthropologists and the accounts of historians. There were, of course, innumerable aspects to the contrast which he thus posited between two basic kinds of society, and already *Division* had explored some of those aspects. In *Formes*, almost twenty years later, Durkheim advanced a relatively narrow and indirect analysis of that contrast, focused on Australian totemism. But, as I indicated, the scope of his argument was very wide, for in his view totemism, as the most primitive form of religion accessible through research, provided the student with privileged insights into the nature itself of the religious experience, not just in that form but in all later, more elaborate ones.

Sacred and Profane

Some of those insights can only be appreciated by placing them against the background of views of the religious phenomenon current in Durkheim's own time, and which he considered as inadequate and sometimes as positively misleading. To begin with, according to him, those views mostly assumed, adopted, or expressly advanced unacceptable definitions of the phenomenon itself, attributing to religion such traits which only some religions possessed in fact—for instance, a reference to a deity. To remedy this state of affairs, Durkheim proposed the following definition, which in his view conveyed what all religions have demonstrably in common:

A religion is a unitary system of beliefs and practices concerning things sacred, that is, set aside, forbidden. Such beliefs and practices unite all those who subscribe to them into the same moral community, called a Church. (F 65; 44)

But again, 'sacred' is one term within a pair of contrasting ones, the other being 'profane'. Before stating that definition, Durkheim had formulated as follows the contrast in question:

All known religious beliefs, whether simple or complex, share a characteristic: they project [*suppose*] a classification of all things, real or ideal, that men represent to themselves, into two contrasting classes or kinds, generally designated by two distinct expressions which the words *profane* and *sacred* translate satisfactorily. The division of the world into two domains, one comprising all that is sacred, the other comprising all that is profane—such is the distinctive trait of religious thought . . . What characterizes this classification of things as against all others is the fact that it is highly peculiar: *it is absolute* . . . The sacred and the profane have always been conceived as separate kinds, as two worlds which have nothing in common. (F 50–1, 53; 34, 36; emphasis original)

Religious practices, accordingly, are in the first place intended to mark, to observe the distinction postulated by religious beliefs; the most significant of them, therefore, express, in however different ways, a basic preoccupation—to keep the two kinds of things apart. They amount to what Durkheim calls 'interdictions', and allow sacred things to be characterized chiefly, as above, as 'set aside, forbidden'.

Are sacred those things which interdictions protect and isolate; are profane those to which those interdictions apply and which must remain at a distance from the former. Religious beliefs are representations which express the nature of sacred things and the relations in which they stand to one another and to profane things. Finally, rituals are rules of conduct which prescribe how man must behave toward sacred things. (F56; 38)

Durkheim's emphasis on the duality of sacred and profane as the core aspect of religion represents a major advance in the study of the religious phenomenon; a few years after *Formes*, Rudolf Otto was to develop independently a similar argument in another work of great significance on that topic, *The Idea of the Holy*.[1] In my view, however, the way Durkheim expressly construes that duality should not be taken at face value. For the great bipartition of all that is known and knowable into a sacred and a profane realm is *itself* the work of religion; the sacred/profane distinction is *itself* a religious distinction.

If so, then religion is not exclusively a set of institutions attending, so to speak, to the sacred half of the universe. In the very moment in which it posits that duality, in order to inscribe itself within that half, it represents, classifies, orders the whole: *both* that half itself *and* the other, profane half. Implicitly, the one side of the bipartition to which religion apparently confines itself *envelops* the other side.

I take this expression from a passage where Durkheim, it seems to me, comes very near acknowledging the point I am making, though the passage in question refers, on the face of it, to *another* duality, that of moral versus material forces. The passage is worth quoting at some length, if only to allow the reader to decide whether it respects or contradicts Durkheim's express view that religion attends to only one side of reality (personally I feel that it contradicts it):

When they make their appearance in history, religious forces present an ambiguity; they are at the same time physical and human, moral and material. They are moral powers, for they are entirely constructed from the impressions awakened by that moral being, the collectivity, within those other moral beings that individuals are . . . Their authority is merely one form of the moral ascendant that society exercises over its members. However, on the other hand, since they are conceived under material forms, they can but be regarded as strictly related to material things. Thus, they dominate the two worlds. They reside within men; but they are, at the same time, the vital principles of things . . . It is thanks to this double nature that religion has been the matrix from which all the main components of human civilization have developed. Since it has found itself *enveloping* within itself the whole of reality, the physical as well as the moral universe, the forces which move the bodies as well as those which lead the spirits have been conceived in religious form. (F 318–19; 224–5; emphasis added)

An apposite example is offered by an Australian tribe from Mount Gabier:

There are ten clans; as a consequence, the whole world is partitioned into ten classes, or rather into ten families, each of which has its root [*souche*] in a special totem . . . Taken together, these ten families of things constitute a complete and systematic representation of the world; and this representation is religious, for it has its principles in religious notions. (F 219; 155)

Thus, I would argue, the sacred/profane partition is asymmetric, in that it assigns an implicit priority to the sacred over the profane part. If this is granted, one may wonder about the reasons for the asymmetry (which Durkheim does not expressly acknowledge). My hunch is that it expresses Durkheim's personal, powerful hankering for unity, evidenced among other things by the positive emotional loading (again unacknowledged) which attaches in his writings to such expressions as 'solidarity' or 'cohesion'.

Inadequate Understandings of Religion

After proposing his own definition of religion, Durkheim criticizes theories of the religious phenomenon which stressed only the component of belief and assigned a derivative, secondary role to ritual. A correct understanding of the phenomenon, in his view, must assign to ritual, we might say, 'equal time', acknowledge the existential significance it has for men and women who live a religious experience:

They sense, in fact, that the true function of religion is not to make us think, to enrich our knowledge, to add to those representations we owe to the sciences others having another origin and another character—but to make us act, to assist us in living ... From this point of view, this set of regularly repeated acts which constitutes a cult regains all its significance ... The cult is not simply a system of signs by means of which faith expresses itself externally, but a collection of means whereby it periodically creates and re-creates itself. (F 595–6; 419–20)

Furthermore, and more significantly, Durkheim attacks all views which consider religion as a set of intrinsically mistaken views and meaningless acts, brought into being by the conditions of ignorance and helplessness prevalent in the early stages of the development of humanity, kept in existence by the persistence of those conditions in the less advanced regions of the earth and within the less enlightened social strata in the more advanced regions, but destined to recede in the face of advancing science and technology.

For instance, according to the doctrine called *animism*, one of the views of the origins and nature of religion which deprive religion of any truth value,

sacred beings would be ... nothing else but imaginary conceptions engendered by man in the course of a kind of delirium ... If he prays, if he makes sacrifices and offerings, if he bears dutifully the manifold deprivations prescribed by ritual, it's only because a constitutional aberration leads him to misconceive his dreams as perceptions, death as a prolonged sleep, dumb objects as living and thinking beings. Thus ... behind all those images and those figures there would be nothing but the nightmares of uncultivated spirits. At bottom, religion would be nothing but a dream, a systematic and lived dream, but without any foundation in reality. (F 97; 65–6)

Durkheim counters those and similar views by arguing the functional indispensability of religion under any social conditions, and grounds in turn that indispensability on the fact that, in their own fashion, *all religions are true*. 'Even if there is reason for saying that no religion dispenses with a kind of delirium, one must add that this delirium ... *is well grounded*' (F 324; 228; emphasis original).

We shall see below how, and in what sense, Durkheim asserts the essential truthfulness of religion. Here we can note in passing that this assertion (as well as others developed in *Formes*) puts him at odds with a whole tradition of social thinking which, in different ways, considers (and condemns) the religious phenomenon as essentially ideological. That is: religion is criticized and rejected as an understanding of human condition which undervalues the humans' intrinsic potentialities, projects them onto beings different from themselves, and thereby prevents or hinders their development. Durkheim explicitly rebukes one of the most ancient arguments to this effect:

One has often attributed the first religious conceptions to a sentiment of weakness and dependence, of fear and of anguish which purportedly seized man when he began to relate to the world ... The earliest religions have a wholly different origin. The famous formula *Primos in orbe deos fecit timor* [fear produced the first gods of the Universe] is in no way justified by facts. The primitive did not see these gods as strangers, as enemies, as essentially and necessarily malevolent beings whose favour he was compelled to win at all costs. Rather they are for him friends, relatives, natural protectors. (F 320; 225)

It is enough to consider early forms of religious life, which are not associated with a division of sacred labour, so to speak, between religious professionals and the laity, to see as flawed another critique of religion as ideology, that goes under the name of the 'priestly lie':

When the eighteenth century philosophers turned religion into a vast error imagined by the priests, they could, at any rate, account for its persistence as due to the priestly caste's interest in deceiving the multitudes. But if the people themselves have fashioned this system of mistaken ideas and at the same time have been misled by them, how could this extraordinary deception prolong itself over the rest of history? (F 98–9; 66)

But the most intellectually weighty view of religion as ideology is that elaborated, in Durkheim's own time, by the followers of Marx under the name of *historical materialism*. Durkheim knew that his own theory of religion ran the risk of being understood as a variant of that view, and was particularly keen to reject such misunderstanding:

By showing religion as essentially a social thing, we do not at all intend to say that all it does is convey, in another language, the material forces of society and its immediate vital needs. Undoubtedly, we consider it obvious that social life depends on its substratum and bears its marks ... but the collective consciousness differs from a simple epiphenomenon of its morphological basis. (F 605; 426)

In fact, in *Formes*, Durkheim modified or qualified his earlier views on the relationship between the morphological substratum of society and its institutional make up. But here we may return to the *positive* side of Durkheim's critique of views of 'religion as ideology': his affirmation of the essential truthfulness of religion as such, indeed of all religions, no matter how 'primitive'.

The basic insight is repeated time and again in *Formes*; I quote below an early formulation, following a critique of two deficient understandings of the nature and origins of religion, animism and naturism:

Since neither man nor nature have, in themselves, a sacred character, it must be the case that they derive it from another source. Outside the human individual and the physical world, there must be some other reality with respect to which that kind of delirium which, in a sense, all religion amounts to, acquires objective meaning and objective value. (*F* 124; *84–5*)

Totemism

Totemism, which Durkheim considers 'another cult, more fundamental and more primitive' (*F* 124; *85*) than those which have inspired both the animist and the naturist theories of religion, offers a basic cue concerning that 'other reality', and thus the essential truthfulness of religion. Totemism, as Durkheim understood it (note that this understanding is currently judged very doubtful; it is highly controversial even whether totemism should be considered a form of religion, elementary or not), is a religion systematically associated with a particular (and highly primitive) form of collective unit—the clan.

This grouping has two basic features: it is composed of individuals who see themselves as tied together by a form of kinship based not on consanguinity, but on a shared name; this name, in turn, designates also a particular kind of material thing (most often an animal, less often a plant, occasionally a place or a feature of the natural environment). The kinship shared among the individuals, with its usual obligations of solidarity, is seen as tying them also to the thing in question. *Totem* is the generic name for this thing; each such thing is the property of the clan as a whole, but also of its members; or, vice versa, both the clan and its members belong to and with the thing in question, its totem.

The totem both 'names' the clan and represents it, is the clan's emblem. Besides being embodied in the single, concrete members of the given class of things (typically, in each animal of the appropriate species), the totem is widely represented in artefacts, sometimes

151

reproduced on the body itself of the clan members, and its origins and doings are the theme of many myths of the clan. But (and this is critical) the totem is not only a name and an emblem; it is also the object of particular practices binding on the clan, beginning (when appropriate) with the prohibition on eating or damaging it. As this suggests, 'it is the type itself of the sacred things', and all further classification of things into sacred and profane is grounded on their relation to the totem.

It is, in particular, because the clan members share the totem's name that 'each is invested with a sacred character'; for 'each man believes he is, not just a man in the ordinary sense of the word, but at the same time an animal or a plant of the totemic species' (F 190; *134*). However, in keeping with his practice of discounting interpretations of collective practices and properties that derive from the repetition and summation of individual ones, Durkheim argues that this sacralization of the individual only reflects his/her participation in the sacred collective, his/her membership in the clan. 'The totemism of the individual comes later than the totemism of the clan and indeed appears to derive from it' (F 268; *190*). The same thing applies to the sacred qualities enjoyed by other things.

What, then, determines the sacredness of the clan totem itself? It cannot be its intrinsic properties, those grounded on the material nature, say, of this or that totemic animal or plant, for the latter's sacredness is, to a greater or lesser extent, shared with other, differently constituted things. This suggests that, quite generally, sacredness is a quality superimposed, *surajoutée* (F 461; *327*), on the object from outside, rather than, flowing from inside it and manifesting itself outside of it. *Whoever* does the superimposing (let us leave this matter open for the time being) must do so in response to a compelling experience, awakening a sense mixed of fear, dependency, trust, awe, that gets then invested in the totemic object and related objects, sacralizing them.

God Is Society

The question then becomes: *what* experience? Durkheim answers it in two steps. First step: the totem is seen as the carrier of something which surpasses it and yet represents itself in it. It is a particular way of conceiving the *mana*, a universal force, which vivifies and unifies all of reality.

Totemism is the religion, not of these animals, or of these men, or of these images, but of a kind of anonymous and impersonal force, to be found in each of those beings, but not to be confounded with them. None possesses the whole of it and all partake of it ... Taking the expression 'god' in a broad sense, one could say that this force is the god which every totemic cult worships. However, it is an impersonal god, without name, without history, immanent in the world, diffused within an innumerable plurality of things ... But the Australian does not represent to himself this impersonal force in an abstract form; he is led to conceive of it under the appearances of an animal or a vegetable, that is of a material thing. Here is what the totem consists in: it is merely the material form under which there is represented to imaginations this immaterial substance, this energy radiating through all manner of heterogeneous beings, which is, alone, the true object of the cult ... What we find at the base and at the root of religious thought are not determinate and distinct objects or beings which in themselves are of sacred character; rather, we find indefinite powers, anonymous forces .... whose impersonality is strictly comparable to that of the physical forces whose manifestations are studied by the sciences of nature. (F 269–70, 285–6; 191, 202)

The second step in Durkheim's argument—the most distinctive and controversial—consists in determining how humans have attained the notion itself of *mana*, 'a semi-divine principle, immanent in certain categories of men and things and conceived under animal or vegetable form'. He reminds the reader that the totem is on the one hand the visible embodiment of the *mana*, on the other 'the symbol of that species of society one calls the clan', and proceeds from this remark, by means of two rhetorical questions, to his central argument:

If [the totem] is, at the same time, the symbol of the god and of the society, could it not be the case that god and society are one and the same thing? How could the emblem of the group become the image of this semi-divinity, if the group and the divinity were two distinct realities? The god of the clan, the totemic principle, cannot then be other than the clan itself, though personified and represented to the imagination under the material appearances of the vegetable or the animal that serves as totem. (F 294–5; 208)

This passage appears more or less in the middle of the book, and from this point on *Formes* seeks chiefly to elaborate and substantiate its argument, suggesting that it holds not only for primitive societies and *their* religions, but for all societies and all religions. Quite generally, the religious phenomenon constitutes a way for society to represent itself to its members and to evoke in its members sentiments appropriate to the relationship in which they stand to it. The *truth* of religion—of all religions—rests on the fact that the referent of religious beliefs and practices is society.

Of course, the reference itself is extremely varied: it is relatively direct in the case of totemism, where the same name designates the totem and the group, and becomes more remote in the case of more advanced religions. In all cases it is of course highly symbolic, for the relationship between the sign (in this case, a given sacred belief or practice) and what is being signified (ultimately, if Durkheim is right, society: its nature, its needs) is utterly arbitrary—as someone has said of ritual acts in particular, they are devoid of sense but full of meaning. The ritual gesture serves as carrier for a message which widely surpasses its immediately intelligible content.

We can never escape the dualism of our nature and free ourselves entirely of physical necessities: in order to express to ourselves our very ideas, we need . . . to attach them to material things which symbolize them. But here, the role performed by nature is minimal. The object which serves as support to the idea is a very minor matter, compared to the ideal superstructure within which it is subsumed. (F 326–7; 229–30)

The necessity of mediating meanings through symbols is all the greater when it is a matter of, so to speak, delivering messages *to* a plurality of individuals *concerning* a plurality of individuals:

One may conceive of individual representations while abstracting from those physical repercussions which accompany them or follow them, but do not constitute them. But it is wholly otherwise with collective representations. These suppose that various consciousnesses act and react the ones upon the others; they are the upshot of these actions and reactions, which in turn are possible only through material intermediators . . . Without symbols, social sentiments could only live a precarious existence . . . But if the movements by means of which these sentiments have found expression come to be inscribed upon durable things, the sentiments themselves become durable . . . Thus the emblematism necessary for society to become conscious of itself, is no less indispensable in order to guarantee the continuity of this consciousness. The fact itself that thus collective sentiments become attached to things which are foreign to themselves . . . does nothing but express in sensible form a real feature of social facts, their transcendence with respect to individual con-sciousnesses . . . Social life, in all its aspects and in all moments of its history, is only possible thanks to a vast symbolism. (F 330–1; 232–3)

Note that Durkheim speaks of symbolism in a strong sense, as a relationship between signifier and signified which is *particularly* arbitrary and, to that extent, creative. This—it seems to me—is implied in a footnote in *Formes* where he comments on his own statement that, as the members of *its* clan consider it, 'the kangaroo ... contains in itself a principle which sets it aside from the other beings in the environment, and this principle does not exist except in the minds that think it' (F 492–3; *349*). The footnote reads:

In a philosophical sense, the same applies to everything, for nothing exists except through its representation. But, as we have shown, this proposition is doubly true of religious forces, since, in things as they are constituted, there is nothing that corresponds to the sacred character. (F 493 n. 1; *349 n. 55*)

Society Is God

In its sharpest formulation, Durkheim's main thesis about religion is 'God is society'. The parts of *Formes* which seek to substantiate this thesis do so chiefly by developing the obverse one: 'Society is God'. That is: society by its very nature is uniquely suited to inspire those sentiments which, focused on something outside themselves, constitute this something as God—although, in its primitive form, the God in question is conceived not as a self-standing, personal being, but as a pervasive, universal, impersonal force: the *mana* which in turn represents itself, to a given clan, as its totem.

To qualify as God, as it were, society presents in *Formes* a somewhat different image from that I have sketched in Chapter 5. Durkheim's emphasis, in this new image, lies less on the normative constraints constitutive of society, to be observed in a spirit of dutiful obligation by its members, and more on the energy society generates, on the sentiments it inspires, in those members. Society is presented less as a norm, or as a set of norms, and more as a force, or a set of forces. It appears less as a constituted reality confronting individuals, more as the process which constitutes such a reality, and does so by involving the individuals themselves as participants, rather than as the addressees of commands. To return to the concepts mentioned at the beginning of this chapter, the society's members are envisaged chiefly as the carriers of *états forts de conscience*, and those states that do not qualify as such remain largely unlabelled and unthematized.

In sum, society undergoes in *Formes* a process of transfiguration which renders it unmistakably fit to be sacralized and deified. Religion necessarily becomes its mirror, the source of its identity, the sole adequate expression of its greatness and might, the chief medium and propellant of individuals' continuous enactment and renactment of society itself. All other institutions, from science to law to the family, appear chiefly as offshoots, elaborations of *the* institution *par excellence*, religion itself. Even the two halves of the 'twofold man', otherwise theorized by Durkheim in earlier works, reappear now as respectively a sacred and a profane component. (*F* 376; 265–6)

I have emphasized what seem to me the distinctive new components of Durkheim's image of society in *Formes*, even if some of them had been foreshadowed in earlier work. For instance, in comparing his own view of morality with Kant's, Durkheim had criticized the latter for overemphasizing the component of dutifulness, of obligation in moral conduct.[2] But

it is necessary that side by side with its obligatory side the moral end [*la fin morale*] should be desired and desirable. . . . One could show that, even within obligation, pleasure and desirability enter; we experience a certain appeal [*charme*] when we carry out the moral act commanded to us by the norm, and just because it is commanded. We experience a *sui generis* pleasure when we do our duty, because it is our duty. (*S&P* 62–3; 45)

However, this image of society as a reality whose norms exercise attraction and engender desire and indeed pleasure for the individual must accommodate other aspects of society discussed in Chapter 5 above, and the attendant problems.

To some extent, what I have called a process of transfiguration of society in *Formes* (a less benevolent label might be 'a process of *transmogrification*') flows from Durkheim's decision to concentrate his attention on the dynamics of Australian clan society. It is doubtful, according to current criticism, whether he used the right sources to derive from them his own view of the aboriginal clans, or whether he interpreted rightly those sources. But there is little doubt that he grounded in them a powerful, compelling vision of the makings and operations of what he rightly or wrongly judged to be the most primitive societies accessible to scientific inquiry. There is also little doubt that he amplified that vision into a general, comprehensive conception of social dynamics at large, where ritual ceremonies, which *Formes* describes at length and most eloquently, become *the* paradigmatic collective experience, the time and place where society can be apprehended *in statu nascendi*, and *états forts de conscience* are, so to speak, the name of the game.

Rituals

What do we see as we observe, through Durkheim's eyes as it were, an Australian clan's ritual ceremony being performed? In the first place, what we might call the chorality of the experience: the actions of the individual participants merge into

a single outcome ... which conveys to those individuals that they are at unison and that it behoves them to become aware of their moral unity. It is by virtue of screaming the same cry, pronouncing the same word, performing the same gesture concerning the same object that they achieve and experience an accord ... It is the homogeneity of these movements which imparts to the group the sense of its identity [le sentiment de soi] and consequently makes it be. (F 329–30; 232)

In the second place, according to Durkheim's consistently anti-individualistic interpretation of social facts, mostly such gestures do not so much express a sentiment previously existent within each individual as themselves symbolize and perhaps generate such a sentiment. Suppose we are watching a funeral ceremony, which may comprise a number of loud, violent, sometimes shocking expressions of sorrow; typically, according to Durkheim,

the sorrow [deuil] is not the spontaneous expression of individual emotions. If the relatives cry, complain, hurt themselves, this does not mean that they feel personally touched by the death of their relative ... Mostly, there is no relationship between the sentiments experienced and the gestures performed by those taking part in the ritual ... The sorrow is not a natural motion of private sensitivity, offended by a cruel loss; it is a duty imposed by the group. (F 567–8; 400)

In any case, the sorrow expressed ritually has in common with different ritual gestures, also performed in response to group expectations, the property of generating among the participants 'a state of effervescence' (F 571; 403): that is, a heightening of emotions, a sense of release from ordinary cares and constraints, an intense involvement, a sense that the experience the participants share is a significant one, one out of the ordinary.

We may also observe a number of arrangements, all of them prescribed by the cult itself, which make it easier for this particular state to be attained. In the first place, all of the members of the clan, or of a particular portion of it, may be assembled in a small place: in other terms, to go back to the expressions used in Division, the material density of the occasion is relatively high. But so is the moral density, because the assembled people, as indicated, interact intensely, each of them making him/herself accessible to all others and seeking contact with them. The intensity they experience may be variously enhanced: for instance, the assembly may take place at night, in the light of a single bonfire, placed in the middle of the space; the participants may be drugged or intoxicated, and thus capable of emotions surpassing those of their mundane existence. The bodies of many of them exhibit the tattooed image of the totem, and some may be wearing special apparel or masks, which distance them from their everyday appearance and transfigure them. As we have seen, the participants chant, dance, gesture, scream in unison. They appear possessed, prey to tumultuous emotions not of their own making, but generated by the fact and the manner of their being assembled. They celebrate the totem, and their own oneness with it, by recounting and re-enacting its mythical feats. They reconsecrate themselves to it, to the clan, to one another.

As a result of all these arrangements, the individuals involved experience themselves exclusively in their capacity as clan members, as parts of a whole which grounds and dignifies their existence, confers upon them extraordinary powers, and merges their acts into the action of a single, collective subject. Their *états forts de conscience* are a product of the performance of a pre-existing script, and induce them in turn to revisit, and to re-commit themselves to, other aspects of the clan's lore.

However, according to Durkheim, as we have seen at the beginning of this chapter, this situation opens a vista on a different, primeval, creative condition, where similar *états forts* generate new lore, institute new manners of acting and thinking, project and validate new visions, establish the primordial identity of the clan with its totem. In this manner, thanks to the extraordinary intensity of such a condition, the intrinsically divine nature of society is envisaged and affirmed. (The notion of 'liminality', introduced into contemporary anthropological and sociological discourse by Victor Turner, is related to this conception.)[3]

But it was Durkheim's conviction that the relationship he had established (to his own satisfaction) between the most elementary form of religion—totemism—and the most elementary form of society—the clan—could be predicated of all religions and all societies, although the complexity of the relationship could be expected to vary with the complexity of those two terms. Thus his argument mixes considerations directly concerning his Australian database, as we would call it today, with others of the greatest generality.

Here, I emphasize the second level of discourse, and attempt to specify what qualities of society *as such*, according to Durkheim, could inspire the notion of divinity. For, as he says, 'In quite general terms, there is no doubt that a society has all that is required to awaken within the spirits [of humans], just through the action it exercises upon them, the sensation of the divine' (F 295; 208). In the following paragraphs, I will paraphrase the way he himself articulates this bold statement.

To begin with, a god is a being which humans represent to themselves as superior to themselves and on which they depend. In their quality as believers, they see themselves as having dealings with the god, and they owe to it to observe the ways of acting it imposes on them. But humans relate in the same way to the society of which they are members: it has ends of its own, but can only attain them by laying claims on the members and constraining their activities to observe rules of conduct and of thought of its own making, often contrasting with those the members would spontaneously adopt if left to themselves.

Gods are conceived, essentially, as moral powers, for their commandments do not impose themselves on the faithful with the inexorable cogency of laws of nature. The same thing can be said of society's claims: 'the empire it exercises on consciousnesses owes much less to the physical supremacy which it enjoys than to the moral authority vested in it. If we defer to its commands, it is not simply because it is armed in such a way as to overcome our resistance; it is, primarily, because it is the object of veritable respect' (F 296; 209).

Respect is the emotion we experience when, exposed to someone else's commands, we sense within ourselves a pressure of a wholly subjective nature, which induces us to disregard how convenient and advantageous (or inconvenient and disadvantageous) it would be for us to observe those commands. Instead, we consider their source, and we bow to the authority of the latter.

'But a god is not only an authority on which we depend; it is also a force on which our own force rests' (F 299; 211); it infuses the faithful one with confidence and energy in his/her dealings with the world. Similarly, society does not simply lay claims upon its members from outside, but penetrates them and organizes itself within them; it raises them and nurtures them. This action is particularly intense in extraordinary circumstances, whose risks and opportunities seem to draw from individuals, in so far as they communicate intensely with one another, capacities of which they were not aware, and which display themselves in unprecedented collective feats. More generally, those who comply with society's demands are repaid, so to speak, with an enhanced sense of their own moral worth.

But society visits upon its members other benefactions, of such significance as to make it appear more and more divine:

We speak a language not of our making; we employ devices not invented by us; we appeal to rights we have not instituted; on each generation is bestowed a treasure of knowledge it has not itself gathered, and so on. It is to society we owe these varied goods of civilization: and . . . man is not such except because he is civilized . . . Thus, he could not escape feeling that there are outside of him forces from which derive the characteristic features of his nature, and benevolent powers which assist him, protect him and assure him of a privileged position. To such powers he could but assign a dignity in keeping with the high value of the goods he attributed to it. (F 303; 214)

Thus, humans find themselves in relation to forces 'at the same time imperious and succouring, majestic and benevolent', which can inspire in them the appropriate sentiment of respect if they have been 'metamorphosed' by religion; while they can relate to other forces in a mundane manner, purely as they manifest themselves to the senses.

As a consequence, we have the impression that we stand related to two distinct kinds of reality, separated by a sharply drawn line of demarcation: on the one side, the world of profane things, on the other that of sacred things. (304; 214)

This distinction finds expression both in the different postures that people adopt in dealing with both realms (gingerly, cautious, and deferent in one case, matter-of-fact in the other) and in the qualitative difference between sets of ideas relating to each: some are protected from doubt and criticism, treated as intrinsically right and true; others can be the object of legitimate doubt and experimentation.

As can be seen from these considerations (closely based on a section of *Formes*, 295–305; 208–15), Durkheim's conception of society, in his last masterpiece, is wider than that I have attributed to him in Chapter 5 above. Principally, of course, it differs in that it develops what one might call the double equation God/society (God is society; society is God); quite literally, it sacralizes society. But with this major difference are associated a few new emphases: the significance of *états de conscience*, and their duality; the indispensability of symbolism; the empowering, as against the constraining, effects of society upon individuals.

Also, Durkheim's vision of society in *Formes* is enriched by an extensive and imaginative argument (to which I cannot here devote the space it deserves) about the specifically intellectual aspects of society's operations. In *Formes*, much more expressly than in other writings (except a major essay written with Marcel Mauss about 'primitive forms of classification'[4]), Durkheim envisages society as generating, and as functioning through, what the French would call *cadres mentaux*, 'mental frameworks'.

In particular, he daringly revisits the philosophical controversy about 'categories' (basic ways of conceiving time, space, cause, class, unity, plurality, etc.), and argues his dissent both from those who see them as constitutive, innate properties of the human mind, grounding a priori the very possibility of experience, and from those who consider them instead as products of that experience. In his view, the categories are indeed bestowed upon the individual mind prior to experience and as an instrument to it, but they are, themselves, collective properties and reflect collective experience. The bestowing, as it were, is not done by innate human nature but by the group, through socialization; and the specific content of the collectively bestowed ways of conceiving of time, space, causality, class, etc. reflects in turn the way the group institutionally organizes its own time and space, understands causality, classifies objects, and so on.

Social time, social space, social classes, collective causality stand at the base of the corresponding categories, for it is under their social form that the different relations were first apprehended with a certain clarity by human consciousness. (F 633; 445)

This argument makes a most imaginative and inspiring contribution to the sociology of knowledge; but I shall not discuss it here, for it has not much to do with the central argument in *Formes*, which concerns what I called the double equation God/society. This image of society differs on a number of significant points from that outlined in Chapter 5; but it does so chiefly by adding new emphases to that image, rather than modifying it significantly. In any case, it fully confirms it as concerns one essential point, what I have called the contingent nature of society and the attendant *pathos*.

161

Durkheim's Pathos Again

As we have seen, in *Formes* Durkheim sacralizes society, loads it with extraordinary energies, and projects it as all-powerful and beneficient. Individuals owe everything to it. Yet, by the same token, he sees society itself as thoroughly dependent for its very survival on the activity (and in a sense on the goodwill) of individuals. This argument is once more based on what I have called the double equation God/society, and Durkheim develops it chiefly in criticizing one aspect of Robertson Smith's theory of ritual sacrifice. Smith, a very imaginative and profound student of early Semitic religion, had discounted as absurd one aspect of that religion, the fact that on the face of it sacrifices were ways for the faithful to feed the gods, to keep them in existence. For, as the believers' existence depended on the gods, how could the gods' own existence be made to depend on the faithful's sacrificial obeisances?

Durkheim refused to see this as an untenable contradiction, and took on board the circularity of the relationship between the faithful and their gods.

If it is true that man depends on his gods, the dependency is reciprocal. The gods, too, need man [*Les dieux, eux aussi, ont besoin des hommes*]: without the offerings and the sacrifices, they would die . . . (F 52–53; 36)

The circle on which Smith remarks is thus very real: but it entails no defeat for reason. It comes from the fact that sacred beings, superior as they may be to men, cannot live except within human consciousnesses. (F 495; 351)

But this is just a metaphorical expression for an underlying dependency: the godliness itself of the gods is bestowed upon them by the faithful, depends fully on the faithful behaving as faithful, that is, treating the gods as sacred. 'Sacred beings do not exist except because they are represented as such within the minds. Let us cease to believe in them, and they will be as if they did not exist' (F 492; 349).

Note now a redoubtable implication of the double equation God/society: society itself has an existence contingent upon the conduct of its members. Much as it enthuses about the greatness and powerfulness of society, *Formes* also contains a dire prediction of its (possible!) vanishing, which expresses dramatically what I have called Durkheim's *pathos*; this comes toward the end of the following lengthy passage, stating much of the argument I have drawn from *Formes* in this chapter:

In effect, just like [ritual life], social life moves within a circle. On the one hand, man derives from society the best of himself, all that gives him a physiognomy and a place distinct from that of other beings, his intellectual and moral culture. Take away from man language, science, the arts, moral beliefs, and he drops to the level of animals. Thus, the distinctive attributes of human nature come to us from society. Yet, on the other hand, society does not exist and live except within and through individuals. Let the idea of society go out within individual minds, let the beliefs, the traditions, the aspirations of the collectivity cease to be felt and shared by individuals, and *society will die.* One may thus say of it what was said earlier of divinity: it has no reality except to the extent that it holds a place within human consciousness, and it is up to us to make this place for it. Now we descry the profound reason why the gods can no more dispense with their faithful than the latter can dispense with their gods. The reason is that society, of which the gods are but the symbolic expression, can no more dispense with individuals than these can dispense with society. (*F* 495–96; *351*; emphasis added)

This gives clear expression to Durkheim's *pathos*, his sense of the inescapable fragility of society. But the expression differs somewhat in tone from the way I have construed that same *pathos* in Chapter 5, where my focus on normative structures led me to emphasize their intrinsic vulnerability to deviance. In the quote above, Durkheim's focus is on 'the idea of society . . . the beliefs, the traditions, the aspirations of the collectivity' which may 'cease to be felt and shared by individuals'. The difference is associated with the accentuated idealistic tone of *Formes*, explicit in the following passage among others:

For society is not simply constituted by the mass of the individuals who compose it, by the territory they occupy, by the things they make use of, by the movements they carry out, *but primarily by the idea of itself which it makes itself.* And of course it happens that it hesitates concerning the way in which it must conceive itself: it feels pulled this way and that. But these conflicts, when they explode, take place not between the ideal and reality, but between two different ideals, yesterday's and today's, that backed by the authority of tradition and that in the process of becoming. It is of course perfectly legitimate to inquire into why ideals evolve; but whatever solution one finds to this problem, it remains the case that *everything goes on within the world of the ideal.* (*F* 604; *425*; emphasis added)

Other indications of Durkheim's idealistic turn are his expressed rejection of a historical-materialist interpretation of his views on religion, his reluctance to assign a serious causal role to what (in spite of that) he continues to call the 'substratum' of society (*F* 327, n. *1; 230, n. 41*), and something I have already remarked on. That is:

the prevalent imagery of society is no longer focused on institutional structures, on embodied manners of acting and thinking, but on the tone, fervid or cool, of states of mind. Put this way, Durkheim seems to visualize society less and less as a set of scripts or blueprints, more and more as an atmosphere.

An Answer to the Pathos

For all this, the concern with the fragility of society, the acute sense of its inescapably problematical nature, is common to *Formes* and to previous writings. *Formes*, however, as I read this text, implies an imaginative solution to the problem, nowhere explicitly articulated by Durkheim, and which I would like to outline.

Put very simply, the problem lies in the temptation which besets individuals to misbehave, to disregard the claims laid upon them by society, especially via its normative structures, and to antepose their egoistic interests or whims to society's demands and requirements. It is true that Durkheim rejects a crude individual/society contrast and calls for their interpenetration—he states, for instance, that 'society can exist only if it penetrates the consciousness of individuals'[5]; but he reintroduces the contrast, among other things, by speaking of 'twofold man'.

When all is said and done, what we are up against is every man's reluctance to do his duty, to abide by the dictates of society. How can this be curbed? A solution might be sought in the fact that individuals are not only recalcitrant addressees of the society's commands; they are also, in a different capacity, the sources and authors of those commands. If they could be induced to hear in them their own voice, this might temper their reluctance; what they lose in terms of their individual preferences, which they often must disregard or override in complying with the commands, they would gain in seeing affirmed, realized, the preferences they have expressed as members of society.

I think this solution is implied in one of the several diverse statements Durkheim gave in his thesis about the 'twofold man', a statement found in *Formes*: 'Everything goes on as if we really had two souls: one, which is within us, or rather is us; the other that lies above ourselves, and whose function consists in controlling and assisting the former' (F 402; 283). Durkheim derives this insight from his review of anthropological theories of the origins and nature of the soul. But another possible source of it might have been the political theory of Rousseau (an author Durkheim knew well), and particularly the difference it establishes, in the search for the grounding of republican politics, between *volonté de tous* and *volonté génerale*.

Whereas Rousseau sought to devise constitutional arrangements to ensure the superiority of the general will over that of all, Durkheim sought in religion the solution of a similar problem. However, in one of the passages in which he comes closest to formulating this answer to his own *pathos*, he suggests a strong analogy between properly religious and some properly political occasions:

> There can be no society that does not sense the need to entertain and reaffirm, at regular intervals, the collective sentiments and ideas which constitute its unity and its identity [*personnalité*]. Now, this moral remaking cannot be attained by other means than by gatherings, assemblies, congregations where individuals, brought closely together, reaffirm in common their common sentiments; hence, ceremonies which, as regards their object, the results they produce, the procedures they employ, do not differ in nature from properly religious ones. What essential difference is there between an assembly of Christians celebrating the main dates of Christ's life, or of Jews celebrating the exodus from Egypt or the promulgation of the decalogue, and a gathering of citizens commemorating the institution of a new moral charter or a great event in the life of the nation? (F 610; 429)

Whatever their analogies to different occasions, how do religious rituals manage, as it were, to play up the collective soul of each individual and play down his/her other soul, so that the sacrifice undergone by the latter, its restriction, is compensated by the former's affirmation, its expansion? The basic answer is offered by Durkheim's depiction of clan ritual, and particularly of the key effect we have noted above: individuals' participation in the ritual sublimates their mundane concerns, melts away their ordinary identities, transfigures them by making them experience and express only the visions, feelings, memories, sensations each individual shares with all other participants.

I have said in Chapter 5 that for Durkheim the key mechanism for the maintenance of society is the individual's self-transcendence. *Formes* argues, essentially, that such a feat is not possible for the individual alone. Only the intensely experienced, transporting presence of others and participation with others supplies the individual with, so to speak, a sky-hook for the feat.

It is difficult to see whether and how this way of motivating the individual's compliance with the claims laid upon him/her by society can be applied to social and cultural circumstances different from tribal society. Even if the way in which I have construed Durkheim's implied answer to his own *pathos* is conceptually plausible, its generalizability is very doubtful. If his thinking did take the direction I have imputed to him, it might have increased his sense of estrangement with respect to societies which could not, as effectively as clan societies could, bring their members to experience vividly and compellingly their oneness with one another. Could this be why he claimed to feel more at home in small, close, remote, primitive societies, which he had never directly experienced, than in the society he inhabited?

In any case, not only in *Formes* but in other writings, when Durkheim expressly trains his sights on contemporary societies, some of his thinking could be paraphrased and parodied, in the manner of *My Fair Lady*, as 'Why can't Frenchmen | be more like Bushmen?'. Two things, I feel, keep him from adopting too clearly the plaintive tone characteristic of those speakers who systematic-ally extol the times of old and berate the present ones—and, so to speak, keep his *pathos* from *bathos*: on the one hand, his sense that he has scientifically uncovered requirements of social life so general, and so abiding, that *even* contemporary societies cannot help conforming with them; on the other, a sense of hope *malgré tout*.

I have quoted above a passage containing the prediction 'society will die', *la societé mourra*. This is not a proper prediction, because it is enunciated as the hypothetical result of a condition feared, but not certain: 'Let the idea of society go out in individual minds ... and society will die.' There is, however, a later passage which is a proper prediction, indeed a prophecy, but a hopeful one:

The old gods are ageing or dying, and other ones are not being born ... But this condition of uncertainty and agitation could not last forever. *A day will come* when our societies will experience anew hours of creative effervescence during which new ideals will develop, new ideas will emerge which will, for a time, provide humanity with guidance ... There are no gospels that are immortal and there is no reason to believe that humanity is, at this point, incapable of conceiving new ones. As to knowing in what symbols the new faith will find expression, whether they will be more adequate to the reality which they aim to convey—that is a question which surpasses the human capacity for previ-sion and which, in any case, is not fundamental. (F 610–11; 429–30, emphasis added)

In a less prophetic mode, however, Durkheim seeks, in various writings, to engage the question of the role and content of religion under modern conditions. Two results of that engagement may be mentioned.

A New Religion?

First, Durkheim discounts the significance of something his contemporaries made much of, the conflict between religion and science, which most supposed spelt doom for religion. Durkheim had a very complex and subtle understanding of the relations between religion and science. He refused to see in the former an immature and primitive form of the latter, to be made dispensable by the advance of its mature and sophisticated forms. On the other hand, as we have seen, he did attribute to religion a 'truth value' of sorts, as a symbolic rendering and affirmation of the reality and power of society. According to him, furthermore, the practice of science was only possible on the assumption that nature and other aspects of reality made sense, and that such sense could be apprehended through intellectual effort; but that assumption was itself religious in nature. (In fact, as he repeatedly stated, not just science but *all* institutions, from law to government to the family to science, had emerged from a single institutional matrix—religion itself.) Thus, according to Durkheim, the so-called conflict between religion and science could be solved if religion relieved itself of all the cognitive (he called it 'speculative') baggage it had acquired prior to science reaching maturity and asserting its own autonomy , and went on practising its specific institutional identity as an ensemble of properly religious beliefs and practices, with society as their ultimate referent.

In a more positive mode, Durkheim sought repeatedly to determine what content a modern religion could take, and, more specifically, what aspect of reality it would invest with sacred quality. He took his guidance from previous religious evolution, and particularly from the advance constituted by the advent of Christianity, in his judgement, over earlier forms of religion such as Judaism. Christianity had established the human person as the religious subject *par excellence*, devaluing the qualities it possessed as a member of a specific grouping, envisaging it in its universal significance as a being needful and capable of redemption and as the object of God's love. This advance had continued with reformed Christianity, which had appealed to the individual's capacity for autonomous religious belief and practice and asserted the individual's responsibility for his/her own salvation. With the progress of modernity, the human person had come to be seen as intrinsically vested with rights, which the political community had subsequently expressly proclaimed and institutionalized. (In the name and in defence of such rights Durkheim made his only express intervention in French political conflict, on the occasion of the Dreyfus affair.)

But as the holder of inviolable rights, the person was intrinsically being treated and protected as a sacred object: everybody, *qua* person, possessed some measure of sacredness, and by the same token was expected to respect it in all others. Thus the progress of modern institutions, by conferring rights upon the individual, had identified a new sacred centre for society as a whole, the addressee of a novel sort of cult. The ravages of unbound, egoistic individualism could be moderated and redressed without renouncing the moral progress associated with modernity, by developing institutions which validated the moral significance of *each* individual, and by the same token protected *all* individuals and surrounded them with a halo of respect.

It is important to acknowledge this aspect of Durkheim's view of modernity and of its moral prospects, for it balances out somewhat the views he voiced fairly explicitly and frequently. These on the whole, particularly as Durkheim grew older, were less positive, and more pessimistic, and/or proposed new arrangements (in particular, as we have seen, occupational bodies endowed with public powers) the design of which paid rather less attention to the question of individual rights, and had conservative overtones.

In the context of the discussion of religion, his proposal that the advance of individualism could be crowned by investing it with sacred significance, thus neutralizing its negative moral and social effects, strikes me as somewhat implausible. But there is no doubting the sincerity and earnestness of the moral fervour which inspired it in Émile Durkheim.

Notes

A Scholar's Life and Its Context

1. On the question of Durkheim's relationship to Judaism, see W. S. Pickering, 'The Enigma of Durkheim's Jewishness', in W. S. Pickering and H. Martins (eds.), *Debating Durkheim* (London, Routledge, 1994), 10–39; S. G. Mestrovic, *Emile Durkheim and the Reformation of Sociology* (London, Routledge, 1991), ch. 2; J.-C. Filloux, *Durkheim et le socialisme* (Geneva, Droz, 1977), ch. 1.

2. His adversaries held against Durkheim also the fact that, early in his career, he had conducted research in Germany, and invested much effort in familiarizing himself with the literature on society and culture being produced there. See n. 3 below.

3. On the significance of Durkheim's early research visit to Germany, see R. A. Jones, 'La Science positive de la morale en France: les sources allemandes de *La Division du travail social*', in P. Besnard, M. Borlandi, and P. Vogt (eds.), *Division du travail et lien social: La thèse de Durkheim un siècle après* (Paris, PUF, 1993).

4. A. Giddens, 'Introduction' to *Durkheim on Politics and the State* (Cambridge, Polity Press, 1986), p. 13.

5. See T. Parsons, *The Structure of Social Action* (New York, McGraw-Hill, 1937); S. Hughes, *Consciousness and Society* (London, McGibbon & Kee, 1959).

6. Cf. C. Tarot, *De Durkheim à Mauss, l'invention du symbolique: Sociologie et science des religions* (Paris, La Découverte, 1999).

7. See A. Giddens, *Capitalism and Modern Social Theory: An Analysis of the Writings of Marx, Durkheim and Max Weber* (Cambridge, Cambridge Univ. Press, 1971); and *Emile Durkheim* (London, Fontana, 1971); also the essays on Durkheim in *Politics, Sociology and Social Theory: Encounters with Classical and Contemporary Writings in Social Theory* (Cambridge, Polity Press, 1985). Note also two influential collections of writings by Durkheim edited by Giddens: Emile Durkheim, *Selected Writings* (Cambridge: Cambridge Univ. Press, 1972) and *Durkheim on Politics and the State* (Cambridge, Polity Press, 1986).

8. S. Lukes, *Emile Durkheim, His Life and Work: A Historical and Critical Study* (London, Allen Lane, 1973). Lukes also edited, with A. Scull, *Durkheim and the Law* (Oxford, Robertson, 1983).

9. F. Pearson *Radical Durkheim* (London, Unwin Hyman, 1989). See also M. Gane (ed.), *The Radical Sociology of Durkheim and Mauss* (London, Routledge, 1992), and M. S. Cladis, *A Communitarian Defense of*

Liberalism: Emile Durkheim and Contemporary Social Theory (Stanford, Calif., Stanford University Press, 1992).

10. See M. Gane, 'Durkheim: Woman as an Outsider', in Gane, *Radical Sociology*, 132.

11. See J. M. Lehmann, *Durkheim and Women* (Lincoln, University of Nebraska Press, 1994).

12. See M. Emirbayer, 'Useful Durkheim', *Sociological Theory*, 14 (2) (July 1996), 109–30; C. Tilly, 'Useless Durkheim', in *As Sociology Meets History* (New York, Academic Press, 1981), 95–108. See also M. Emirbayer, 'Durkheim's Contribution to the Sociological Analysis of History', *Sociological Forum*, 12 (2) (1966), 263–83.

13. See J. Chriss, 'Durkheim's Cult of the Individual as Civil Religion: Its Appropriation by Erving Goffman', in *Sociological Spectrum*, 13, (1993), pp. 251–75.

14. K. Erikson, *Wayward Puritans* (New York, Wiley, 1966).

15. F. Alberoni, *Movement and Institution* (New York, Columbia University Press, 1984).

16. D. Lockwood, *Solidarity and Schism: 'The Problem of Order' in Durkheimian and Marxist Sociology* (Oxford, Clarendon Press, 1992).

17. Cladis, *A Communitarian Defense of Liberalism*, esp. ch. 9.

18. See J. Alexander and S. Seidman (eds.), *Culture and Society* (New York, Cambridge Univ. Press, 1990). See also, J. Alexander, 'Rethinking Durkheim's Intellectual Development: On the Complex Origins of a Cultural Sociology', repr. in P. Hamilton (ed.), *Emile Durkheim: Critical Assessments*, i (London, Routledge, 1990), 355–83.

19. See J. Alexander, *Theoretical Logic in Sociology* (Berkeley, Calif., University of California Press, 1982–), ii; R. Muench, *Understanding Modernity: Toward a New Perspective Going Beyond Durkheim and Weber* (London, Routledge, 1988).

Nature and Task of the Sociological Enterprise

1. On *Règles* and more generally on Durkheim's methodology see P. O. Hirst, *Durkheim, Bernard and Epistemology* (London, Routledge, 1975); S. Turner, *The Search for a Methodology of Social Science: Durkheim, Weber, and the Nineteenth-Century Problem of Cause, Probability, and Action* (Dordrecht, Reidel, 1986); M. Gane, *On Durkheim's Rules of Sociological Method* (London, Routledge, 1988).

2. A. Giddens, *New Rules of Sociological Method: A Positive Critique of Interpretative Sociologies* (London, Hutchinson, 1976).

3. E. Durkheim, *Le socialisme: sa définition, ses débuts, la doctrine saint-simonienne* (Paris, Alcan, 1928).

4. See E. Durkheim, *Sociologie et philosophie*, 2nd edn. (Paris, PUF, 1963); *Pragmatisme et sociologie: cours inédit*, (Paris, Vrin, 1955).

5. See E. Durkheim, *L'éducation morale* (Paris, Alcan 1925); *Education et sociologie* (Paris, Alcan, 1938); *L'Évolution pédagogique en France*, 2nd edn. (Paris, PUF, 1969).

The Pattern of Social Evolution

1. A. Hawley, *Human Ecology: A Theory of Community Structure* (New York, Ronald, 1950).

2. L. Schnore, 'Social Morphology and Human Ecology', *American Journal of Sociology*, 63 (6) (May 1958), 620–34.

3. N. Luhmann, 'The Differentiation of Society', in *The Differentiation of Society* (New York, Columbia Univ. Press, 1982), 229–54.

4. See e.g. W. S. F. Pickering, *Durkheim's Sociology of Religion* (London, Routledge, 1984), 283 ff.

5. R. Bendix and B. Berger, 'Images of society', in L. Gross (ed.), *Symposium on Sociological Theory* (Evanston, Ill., Row Peterson, 1959).

6. T. Parsons, 'Durkheim's Contribution to the Theory of Integration of Social Systems', in his *Sociological Theory and Modern Society* (New York, Free Press, 1967), pp. 3–34.

7. C. Tilly, 'Useless Durkheim', in his *Sociology Meets History* (New York, Academic Press, 1981), 95–107.

8. A. Giddens, *Capitalism and Modern Social Theory* (Cambridge, Cambridge Univ. Press, 1971).

Deviance

1. See S. Taylor, *Durkheim and the Study of Suicide* (London, Macmillan, 1982).

2. See P. Besnard, *L'Anomie, ses usages et ses fonctions dans la discipline sociologique depuis Durkheim* (Paris, PUF, 1987). Note that Besnard is somewhat critical of the use of the expression both by Durkheim himself and by many later authors.

3. See W. Pope, *Durkheim's Suicide: A Classic Analyzed* (Chicago, University of Chicago Press, 1976).

4. E. Durkheim and M. Mauss, 'De quelques formes primitives de classification', in E. Durkheim, *Journal sociologique* (Paris, PUF, 1969), 395–460.

5. T. Parsons, *The Structure of Social Action: A Study in Social Theory with Special Reference to a Group of Recent European Writers* (New York, McGraw-Hill, 1937).

6. G. Sorel, *Reflections on Violence*, trans. T. E. Hulme, (London, Allen & Unwin, 1915), 30.

7. Besnard, *L'Anomie*, puts this particular footnote to particularly extensive use, while acknowledging that Durkheim himself 'did everything' to minimize the significance of fatalistic suicide.

8. On the relationship between Durkheim's thinking about modern society and that characteristic of the conservative tradition, see S. Fenton, *Durkheim and Modern Sociology* (Cambridge, Cambridge University Press, 1984). According to Fenton, Durkheim was 'in some senses, a radical critic' of modern society.

What Is Society for Durkheim?

1. E. Durkheim, 'Répresentations individuelles et répresentations collectives', in *Sociologie et philosophie* (Paris, PUF, 1973), 47, n. 1 (*Sociology and Philosophy*, New York, Free Press, 1974, 32, n. 1).

2. N. Luhmann, *A Sociological Theory of Law* (London, Routledge & Kegan Paul, 1985).

3. E. Durkheim, *L'Évolution pedagogique en France* (Paris, PUF, 1989).

4. See E. Durkheim, *Education et sociologie* (Paris, PUF, 1973); and *L'Éducation morale* (Paris, PUF, 1978).

5. G. Simmel, *Conflict: Web of Group-Affiliations* (New York, Free Press, 1955).

Law

1. E. Durkheim, *Leçons de sociologie* (Paris, PUF, 1950).

2. See the texts collected and edited by J. Duvignaud: E. Durkheim, *Journal sociologique* (Paris, PUF, 1969). A quick look at the titles of works reviewed by Durkheim, and listed here on pp. 721–5, will indicate how much attention Durkheim's work as a reviewer devoted to contemporary writings on law, sometimes of a fairly technical nature.

3. *Durkheim and the Law*, ed. S. Lukes and A. Scull (Oxford, Martin Robertson, 1983), 3, 5.

4. S. Sheleff, 'From Restitutive Law to Repressive Law: Durkheim's *Division of Labour in Society* revisited', *European Journal of Sociology*, 16, (1975). See the editors' introduction to the collection *Durkheim and the Law* (n. 3 above) for a discussion of this and related arguments.

5. For a critique of this argument, see D. Garland, 'Durkheim's Theory of Punishment: A Critique', in D. Garland and P. Young (eds.), *The Power to Punish* (London, Heinemann, 1983).

6. See the complete reference in Ch. 1, n. 5.

7. In their Introduction to *Durkheim and the Law*, p. 21, Lukes and Scull express doubts about the validity of Erikson's reappraisal of Durkheim's views.

8. 'Deux lois de l'évolution pénale', first published in *L'Année Sociologique*, iv (1899–1900), repr. in E. Durkheim, *Journal sociologique* (Paris, PUF, 1969), 245–72. Translated as 'The Evolution of Punishment', in *Durkheim and the Law*, ed. Lukes and Scull 102–32.

9. *Journal sociologique*, 273; *Durkheim and the Law*, 131.

10. See R. Dahrendorf, 'In Praise of Thrasimacus', in *Essays in the Theory of Society* (London, Routledge & Kegan Paul, 1968).

11. According to F. Pearson, in his *Radical Durkheim* (London, Unwin Hyman, 1989), 109, Durkheim derived from his reading of R. V. Ihering, during a research stay in Germany, an early understanding of law as the object of political struggle, but subsequently forgot this insight.

12. See ibid. 57.

13. M. Weber, *The Agrarian Sociology of Ancient Civilisations* (London, Verso, 1988). (Translation of *Agrarverhaeltnisse im Altertum: Die sozialen Gruende des Untergangs der antiken Kultur.*)

14. O. Williamson, *Markets and Hierarchies: Analysis and Antitrust Implications—A Study in the Economics of Internal Organization* (New York, Free Press, 1975).

15. G. Gorla, *Il contratto: problemi fondamentali trattati con il metodo comparativo e casistico* (Milan, Giuffrè, 1954).

Political Institutions

1. E. Durkheim, *Montesquieu et Rousseau précurseurs de la sociologie* (Paris, Rivière, 1953).

2. E. Durkheim, 'L'individualisme et les intellectuels', *Revue Bleue*, 4th ser., 10 (July 1898), 7–13.

3. B. Lacroix, *Durkheim et la politique* (Montreal, Presses de l'Université de Montréal, 1981); J.-C. Filloux, *Durkheim et le socialisme* (Geneva, Droz, 1977).

4. See e.g. the Introduction to A. Giddens (ed.), *Durkheim on Politics and the State* (Cambridge, Polity Press, 1986). See also S. Seidman, *Liberalism and the Origins of European Social Theory* (Oxford, Blackwell, 1983); H.-P. Mueller, 'Durkheim's Political Sociology' in S. Turner (ed.), *Emile Durkheim: Sociologist and Moralist* (London, Routledge, 1993), 95–110.

5. Giddens, *Durkheim on Politics and the State*.

6. But note the dissent of M. S. Cladis, *A Communitarian Defense of Liberalism: Emile Durkheim and Contemporary Social Theory* (Stanford, Calif., Stanford University Press, 1992), 289.

7. Giddens, Introduction to *Durkheim on Politics and the State*, 24. A similar argument is made in P. Lacroix, *Durkheim et le politique*.

8. Ibid., 207.

9. W. Kornhauser, *The Politics of Mass Society* (Glencoe Ill., Free Press, 1959).

10. For a sociological analysis of this aspect of Durkheim's thought, see H.-P. Mueller, *Wertkrise und Gesellschaftsreform: Emile Durkheims Schriften zur Politik* (Stuttgart, Enke, 1983).

11. P. Schmitter and G. Lehmbruch, *Patterns of Corporatist Policy-making* (London, Sage, 1982)

12. See P. Ceri, 'Durkheim on social action', in S. Turner (ed.), *Emile Durkheim: Sociologist and Moralist* (London, Routledge, 1993), 139–68.

13. J. L. Cohen and A. Arato, *Civil Society and Political Theory* (Cambridge, Mass., MIT Press, 1992).

14. E. Durkheim, *Textes*, ed. V. Karady, iii (Paris, Minuit, 1975), 237.

Religion

1. R. Otto, *The Idea of the Holy: An Inquiry into the Non-Rational Factor in the Idea of the Divine and Its Relation to the Rational* (London, Oxford University Press, 1926).

2. On the relationship between Durkheim's and Kant's thinking concerning morality, see F.-A. Isambert, 'Durkheim's Sociology of Moral Facts', in S. Turner (ed.), *Emile Durkheim: Sociologist and Moralist* (London, Routledge, 1993), 189–203.

3. V. Turner, *The Ritual Process: Structure and Anti-Structure* (London, Routledge & Kegan Paul, 1969).

4. E. Durkheim and M. Mauss, *Primitive Classification* (London, Cohen & West, 1970). Originally published as 'De quelques formes primitives de classification', in *Année Sociologique* 6, (1903).

5. 'The Dualism of Human Nature and Its Social Consequences', trans. C. Blend, repr. in R. Bellah (ed.), *Emile Durkheim on Morality and Society* (Chicago, University of Chicago Press, 1973), 149.

Index

aborigines
    economic pursuits and religion
        144–5
    religious beliefs 148
    see also animism; Australia;
        clans; primitive societies;
        totemism
action, and thought 19–20, 59–62,
    87–8
Alberoni, F. 13
Alexander, Jeffrey 13
altruism 66–7
altruistic suicide 68, 73–6
animism 149
anomic suicide 76–8
anomie 58, 66–7
    and modernity 79–80, 82
    and regulation 76–7
    atmosphere, society as 164
Australia 156
    religious beliefs of aborigines
        148
    ritual ceremony 157
    totemism 142, 153, 159
    see also primitive societies;
        totemism

Bordeaux University 2–3

Carroll, Lewis 83
categories 161
Catholicism
    and suicide 71–2, 81
    view of Durkheim 1–2
    see also religion
causes, and results 27–9
change
    and anomie 79–80
    dynamics of 50
    see also anomie; modernity
civil society 138–40

civilization
    and division of labour 47
    see also modernity; primitive
        societies; society
clans 156
    and religion 166
    and totemism 151–2, 153, 158
    use of ritual 157–8
    see also primitive societies
class
    and criminal law 107
    and law of property 112
    and need to protect market 137
    social conflict tempered by
        occupational groups 134
    see also society
collective
    and individual 30–1
    see also primitive society
collective consciousness
    loss of determinacy of 52–4
    see also religion; representations
communication, and democracy
    129–31
comparative sociology 27
compliance
    concept of 'ought' 90–3
    conformity and imitation 61
    encouraged by ritual 9
    fear of sanctions 89–90
Comte, Auguste 17
concepts, use of in observations
    23–4
conduct see action
conformity, distinct from imitation
    61
consciousness
    states of: religion 141–6
    see also religion; representations
contextuality, social phenomena
    26–7

contingent reality, society as 85–6,
    88–9, 96
contract
    law of 108–9
        consensual 114–16
        religious form 112–14
        social processes 117–18
    and solidarity 49
    see also law
corporatist project, occupational
    groups 134–8
courants 142
crime
    as normal 61–2, 79
    and punishment 103–6
    see also deviance; law; sanctions
Croce, Benedetto 6
crowd, and irrational passions of the
    masses 7
culture 60
    and psychology 86–8

death of society 166
decriminalization 107
democracy 127–9
    civil society 138–40
    and communication 129–31
    dangers of 131–2
    occupational groups 131–8
Descartes, René 87
deviance
    labelling theory 12
    and modernity 79–83
    as normal 79
    suicide as 62–3
    see also crime; law; sanctions;
        suicide
differentiation process
    and integration 55–7
    modernity and the individual 94
    social division of labour 44–5
    utilitarian approach criticized
        46–7
    see also labour, division of
Division du travail (Durkheim)
    civilization 47

collective consciousness 53
contract 49
differentiation 44–5
dynamics of change 51–2
ecological constraints 41
human ecology 38–9
law of contract 108–9
law and punishment 103, 104
law and social solidarity 103
legal phenomena 22
modernity and anomie 82–3
occupational groups 135–6
punishment as expiation 105–6
role of law in society 101
social facts 19
solidarity 48, 50
two aspects of society 67
undisciplined economic life and
    morality 81–3
divorce, as factor in suicide 78
Dreyfus affair 95
Durkheim, Émile
    assessment of the importance of
        politics to his work 121–4
    biography 1–5
    impact of his work on
        contemporaries 11–24
    intellectual contemporaries 5–11
Durkheim on Politics and the State
    (Giddens) 121

ecological arrangements 19
    see also human ecology
economists, approach to
    differentiation process
    criticized 46
economy
    and morality 81–2, 96, 97
    regulation by occupational groups
        131–8
    religion and economic pursuits:
        aborigines 144–5
education, and socialization 91–3,
    94
egoism 66–7, 82
    and self-transcendence 164–7

egoistic suicide 68, 69–72
elite, and democracy 128
emergence, and sui generis 31–3
'empirical', contemporary definition
    17
environment, relationship to
    society 38–42
equity, and law of contract 116
Erikson, Kai 12, 106
ethics *see* morality; norms
evolution
    human development as an aspect
        of 37–57
    see also society
expiation, role of punishment 105
explanations, causes and results
    27–9

facts *see* social facts
feminism, criticism of Durkheim 12
Ferguson, Adam 55
Formes élémentaires (Durkheim)
    109
    ecological constraints 38–9
    sociology of knowledge 87
France
    academic system 3
    changes during Durkheim's life 2
'free examination', Protestantism
    and suicide 81
Freud, Sigmund 6
Fustel de Coulanges, N.D. 110

generalizations, comparative
    sociology 25–7
Giddens, Anthony 11, 15, 57
    centrality of politics for
        Durkheim 121–2
    Durkheim and ideology 4–5
God
    and society 152–6
    see also religion
Goffman, Erving 12
Gorla, Gino 118
government
    and society 106

see also society; state
grief, and rituals 157

happiness, and division of labour
    47
historical materialism 150
human ecology 37–42
    and dynamics of change 50–2
human nature
    individual and collective aspects
        of 30–1
    and rationality 7–11
    see also mankind
human rights *see* individual rights
hunter-gatherers 43
Hunting of the Snark (Carroll) 83

Idea of the Holy (Otto) 147
ideals 163
ideology, and religion 149–51
imitation
    instinct of 60–1
    peripheral to social process 35
individual
    anomie and suicide 76–8
    centrality of 'ought' 90–3
    and collective 30–1
    concept of and development of
        society 124–5
    and division of labour 46–7
    dynamics of change 50
    emphasis upon and egoistic
        suicide 69–72
    norms and sanctions 89–90
    and social process 33–6
    and society 163
    and society as contingent reality
        85–6, 88–9, 96
    'twofold man' 93–5
    see also anomie
individual rights, and the state
    118–20
industrial society 79
    see also modernity
instincts, and society 86
institutions 142

acting and thinking as constituent elements of 20
laws as way of affecting change 22
see also religion; society
integration, and differentiation process 56
interactions, and definition of society 85–6
interdependencies 42
interdictions, sacred and profane 147

Jaurès, Jean 5

Kant, Immanuel 87, 118, 156
kinship
and totemism 151
see also clans; primitive societies
knowledge, sociology of 87, 161

labelling theory, social deviance 12
labour, division of
collective consciousness 52–4
differentiation 44–5, 55–7, 94
dynamics of change 50–2
and solidarity 47–50, 82
utilitarian approach 46–7
Lacroix, P. 124
L'Année Sociologique 3–5, 99
law
and collective consciousness 52–3
contract 108–9, 112–14
contract (consensual) 114–16
crime and punishment 103–6
evolution of criminal law 106–8
property 109–12
repressive and restitutive sanctions 102–3
and sanctions 22–3, 87–8, 102–3, 115
sociology of 99–101
state and individual rights 118–20
see also crime; deviance; sanctions

Le Suicide: Étude de sociologie (Durkheim) 58
aetiological classification of suicide 65
altruistic suicide 74–6
'free examination' and suicide 81
imitation and conformity 60–1
individuality and egoistic suicide 71
moral ideals and suicide 67
progress and suicide 78
relationship and social process 36
religion and suicide 80–1
state as society's brain 127
see also suicide
Leçons de sociologie (Durkheim) 109
democracy 128–9
democracy and communication 131
individual rights 118–19
law of contract (consensual) 114–16
law of contract (religious form) 112–14
nature of social reality 88
religion and law of property 110–12
Les Formes élémentaires de la vie religieuse (Durkheim) 4
animism 149
definition of religion 146
function of religion 150, 151, 160
ideals 163
individual and society 163
politics and religion 165
ritual 149, 157
sacred and profane 146–7, 148, 160
states of consciousness 141, 143–4
totemism 153
Les Règles de la méthode sociologique (Durkheim)
crime as normal 61–2
individual and collective 29–31, 32

morphology 19–20
observations and concepts 23–4
philosophy 17
positivism and rationalism 14–16
representations 21
social facts 19
social morphology 25
social phenomena, explanations
        for 28–9
liminality 158
Lockwood, David 13
Luhmann, Niklas 44, 87
Lukes, Steven 11
    on Durkheim 12

MacIntyre, Alasdair 13
mana 153
mankind
    evolution of 24
    see also human nature
market
    need for protection from
            employees 137
    and solidarity 48
    see also economic pursuits;
            economy; labour, division of
marriage, and suicide 72
Marx, Karl 11, 13
masses, irrational passions of 7–8
materialist perspective, law of
            property 112
Mauss, Marcel 59, 161
mechanical solidarity 48, 102
méchaniste, dynamics of change 50,
        52
mental disorder, as deviance 62
mental images 86–7
Milioukov, P. 138
Millar, John 55
modernity 12
    deviance 79–83
    differentiation process 44–5
        utilitarian approach 46–7
    Durkheim's view of human
            nature 10–11
    individual and society 94–5

morality
    as constraint 9–10
    and economy 81–2
    individual and society 97
    individuality and egoistic suicide
            71
    study of 24
    see also norms
morphology 20, 39
Movement and Institution
        (Alberoni) 13
Muench, Richard 13
mythical imagination, role in
            human thinking 8–9

nationalism, ousts universality in
        World War I 6
New Rules of Sociological Method
        (Giddens) 15
Nisbet, Robert 11
normal, and pathological 26
norms
    anomie 76–8
    concept of 'ought' 90–3
    deviance 66–8
    and the law 103–4
    sanctions 89–90
    as social facts 142
    society as God 156
    see also crime; deviance; law;
            morality; regulation;
            sanctions

obligatory altruistic suicide 74–5
observation, and speculation 23–4
occupation, supersedes territory as
            significant in society 135
occupational groups 132–4
    corporatist project 134–8
optional altruistic suicide 74–5
organic solidarity 47–50, 56, 102
Oriental societies, and suicide
        80–1
'Other' 16–17
Otto, Rudolf 147
'ought', compliance 90–3, 96

pantheism, and suicide 80–1
parenthood, and suicide 72
Pareto, Vilfredo 6
Parsons, Talcott
    differentiation process 56
    intellectual debt to Durkheim 11
    thought and action 60
pathological, and normal 26
phenomena, contextuality of 26–7
philosophy, Durkheim contrasts
        with sociology 16–17, 29
Plato 107
political structures 124–5
politics
    importance of to Durkheim's
        work 121–4
    and power 124
    and religion 165
    weakness of in Durkheim's work
        122, 138
Polynesians, sacred nature of
        property 110
population density, and division of
        labour 51–2
positivism, and rationalism 14–15
pouvoir constituant, and pouvoir
        constitué 143
power
    and criminal law 107
    and politics 124
    see also class
pre-history 43
prestige 21
primitive societies 43
    and altruistic suicide 73
    chiefs and concept of individual
        125
    religion and economic pursuits
        144–5
    religious beliefs of Australian
        aborigines 148
    see also totemism
profane, and sacred 146–8, 160
Professional Ethics and Civic
        Morals see Leçons de
        sociologie

progress
    and anomie 78
    see also modernity
Protestantism, and suicide 71–2, 81
psychical facts, and social facts 31–3
psychology 29–31
    and culture 86–8
    and sociology 33–6
punishment
    nature of 106–7
    see also crime; deviance; law;
        norms; sanctions

Radical Durkheim (Pearson) 12
rationalism, and positivism 14–15
rationality, and human nature 7–11
Rawls, John 13
reality
    represented by ritual 9
    society as 85
    see also contingent reality
reflection, predating science 16
regulation
    and anomie 76–7
    see also anomie; norms
relationship, and social process 36
religion
    animism 149
    definition of 146
    Durkheim's view of 1–2
    effect of division of labour on 53,
        54
    egoism and self-transcendence
        164–7
    function of 148–51
    God and man: interdependency
        162–4
    God and society 152–5, 152–6
    and ideology 149–51
    law of contract 113–14
    law of property 109–12
    and politics 165
    rituals 157–61
    sacred and profane 146–8
    science and modernity 167–8
    states of consciousness 141–6

and suicide 71–2
totemism 151–5
representations 20–1
  cultural and mental image 86–8
  division of labour 52–4
  norms and sanctions 89–90
  religion 154–5
  and sanctions 21–3
  see also religion
repression
  crime and punishment 103–6
  sanction of the law 102–3
  see also crime; deviance; law;
    sanctions
respect, and religion 159
restitution
  and the law 102–3
  law of contract 115
  see also law
results, and causes 27–9
ritual 157–61
  feast 143
  function of religion 148–9
  and law of property 111
  role of 9
  totemism 154
  see also religion
role, socialization 92–3
Roman Law, property 110–12
Rorty, Richard 13
Rousseau, Jean J. 165

sacred 143
  and profane 146–8, 160
  and totemism 152
  see also religion
sanctions
  law of contract 115
  and norms 89–90
  role of 21–3, 87–8
  see also crime; deviance; law
Schnore, Leo 38
science
  and religion 167
  sociology as 14–16
segments, division of society into 40

self-transcendence
  and egoism 164–7
  socialization 91–3
sentiments, importance of 9
Simmel, Georg 6
  individual and society 93–5
Smith, Robertson 162
social conflict
  and criminal law 107–8
  dangers of democracy 131–2
social constructivism 9
  and the law 104
social currents 20
  and sanctions 23
social facts 18–21
  norms as 142
  and psychical facts 31–3
social process
  and contract 117–18
  individualization as 33–6
  and relationship 36
socialism, as unscientific 15
Socialisme (Durkheim) 15
  'Other' 16
socialization, role of education
    91–3, 94
society
  component parts of 39–42
  differentiation 44–7
  division of labour 55–7
  dynamics of change 50–2
  evolution of 42–4
  as God 155–6
  God as 152–5
  and government 106
  human ecology 37–42
  and the individual 85–6, 93–8, 163
  and 'ought' 90–3, 96
  problem of definition 84–6
  and religion 160
  representations 52–4, 86–8
  sacralization of 162–3
  sanctions 88–90
  socially divided 123
  solidarity 47–50
  types of 25–7

see also anomie; class; modernity
sociology
   Durkheim contrasts with
      philosophy 16–17
   establishment of 2–3
   and psychology 33–6
solidarity 47–50, 82
   and the law 102–3
Sorbonne, Durkheim at 4
Sorel, Georges 6
sorrow, and rituals 157
speculation, and observation 23–4
Spencer, Herbert 17, 34–5, 55–6
   individual rights 118
   solidarity 48
   state 126
   utilitarian approach to
      differentiation process
      criticized 46–7
state
   characterized as society's brain
      126–7, 130
   civil society 139
   democracy 127, 128
   divided society 123
   individual rights 118–20
   need for occupational groups
      131–8
   political power 123–4
   political structures 124–5
   threatened by excessive social
      demands 131
Structure of Social Action (Parsons)
   60
sui generis, Durkheim's use of
   31–2
suicide 145
   aetiological classification 63–6
   altruistic suicide 73–6
   anomic suicide 76–8
   as deviance 62–3
   egoistic suicide 69–72
   norms and deviance 66–9
symbolic function, sanctions 90

symbolic thinking, human capacity
   for 9
symbolism
   and new religion 166
   religion 154–5

Tarde, Gabriel 35, 60, 99–100
territorial considerations, decline in
   importance of 135
things, social facts as 18, 19
thought
   and action 19–20, 59–62, 87–8
   role of mythical imagination 9
Thrasimacus 107
Tilley, Charles 12, 57
Tocqueville, Alexis de 12
totemism 142, 146
   and clan 151–2, 153, 158
   God and society 152–5
   see also religion
Turner, Victor 158
'twofold man' 93–5, 164
type-making, comparative sociology
   25–7

units, division of society into 40–1
unity, role of ritual 157
universality, ousted by nationalism
   in World War I 6
utilitarian approach
   criticized 46–7
   economics and progress 96
   regulation of economy 132

vindictiveness, and the law 104–5

Walzer, Michael 13
Wayward Puritans (Erikson) 12, 106
'Web of Group Affiliations'
   (Simmel) 93–4
Weber, Max 6, 11, 100, 112, 141
World War I 5
   universality ousted by
      nationalism 6–7